Danielle's Story

A Daughter's Battle with Aplastic Anemia

by
Shawn M. Williams

Shawn M. Williams

Bloomington, IN

authorHOUSE™
Milton Keynes, UK

AuthorHouse™
1663 Liberty Drive, Suite 200
Bloomington, IN 47403
www.authorhouse.com
Phone: 1-800-839-8640

AuthorHouse™ UK Ltd.
500 Avebury Boulevard
Central Milton Keynes, MK9 2BE
www.authorhouse.co.uk
Phone: 08001974150

First published by AuthorHouse 4/12/2006

ISBN: 1-4259-1988-X (sc)

Printed in the United States of America
Bloomington, Indiana

This book is printed on acid-free paper.

This book is dedicated to:

God, who put all the right people in my path at the right times.
He is my creator and the One who sustains me.

Cole and Casey who never had the chance to know their big sister.
Danielle always wanted to have a brother and sister and she loved
them dearly.
I only wish she had more time with them.

All of the parents who, unfortunately, understand my pain.

Acknowledgements:

I wish to thank the following people. Mark Williams, my husband and best friend. Our love and marriage only grow stronger with each trial we face. Thank you for standing by me always. Alisha Hecht, my sister, who gave me strength when I needed it. Thank you for being more than a sister to me. My mother, Janet Hecht, who drove with me through many nights to the hospital. Patricia Russell, who did the final proofread of the manuscript. Jerry Davis, author, cousin and friend. Thank you for the countless hours you spent on the manuscript. Had it not been for you my book might still be only a dream.

Grandma Jean, Bill Williams, Carole Inman, Vi Faiver, Uncle Lee and Aunt Leora Stedry. Thank you for all the hours spent at the hospital with us.

There were many other people who touched our lives through Danielle's illness. I have not forgotten any of you. Thank you.

Table of Contents

Chapter 1

"Boo" Is Born

I was 19 years old when I became pregnant. It was a little scary because I was so young, but it was exciting, too. I was encouraged by remembering that Mom had been a single mother who raised my sister and me and we were very close to her growing up. One of the big topics in the media at the time was that teenage pregnancy was on the rise. I used to say, "I won't be a teenaged mom because my due date is a month after my twentieth birthday."

My pregnancy was so easy. I did have a little nausea for a few weeks when I was about three months along, but that didn't last long. I still remember the first time I felt the baby move. Who could ever forget those precious first signs of life? Danielle was born August 16, 1989. That was such a proud day for me. She weighed eight pounds eight ounces and had a head full of dark hair. When I pushed the bassinet through the hallway in the hospital, I loved it when people would ask to see my baby. As soon as I held her in my arms I nicknamed her Boo Boo Bear. From then on I always shortened it to Boo. Later, whenever I called her Danielle, she would ask, "Mom why aren't you calling me Boo?"

While she was growing up, Danielle kept me out of trouble. Many of the right decisions I made in my life were made because of her. Times were hard because we didn't have much money and I think that is what made us close to one another. We didn't own a car or a telephone so we spent a lot of time together walking places or going to parks. When we did have a little money, simple things like buying food from McDonald's or having a pizza were a real treat for us. Looking back now I think to myself, "Those were the worst of times for us, but they were the <u>best</u> of times, too."

Danielle had the most beautiful sky blue eyes and her hair was dark brown. She loved wearing skirts instead of pants and enjoyed playing "dress up." She was not a sickly child nor did she get into trouble in school. Oh, we had a few times when I thought that we would never get along or see eye to eye about certain things, but I think every parent goes through periods of that sort with their children. She was always laughing or teasing and often went to friends' houses or had them over to ours.

Sometimes she just felt like being a couch potato and watching her favorite movies. She loved "The Olsen Twins," "Rugrats" and just about any Walt Disney movie. As Danielle grew up, she went from singing "The Barney Song", to country music, to the songs of The Backstreet Boys. I always thought, "I'll never learn these new songs." So I would just listen to Danielle singing along with the radio and think back to when I was that age. Occasionally I did manage to persuade her to listen to a couple of the songs that were from my time.

When Danielle turned eight I met a man named Mark who fell in love with both of us. He and I were married in 1998. Mark and Danielle got along very well. Sometimes she would go out in the garage where Mark was working just to hang out with him. She would tell him about things that happened in school that day or talk about something that was bothering her. I really liked that they could be close in that way. Sometimes a daughter can't talk to her mom about certain things and needs a father figure to confide in.

Danielle always wanted a sister or brother. After she was older, I decided I wouldn't have any more children because there would be a big age difference between the two of them; but, I guess, you never know how your future will turn out. Mark didn't have any children of his own and he really wanted to be a father. After talking about it, he changed my thinking and we decided to have a baby together

Danielle was very excited when I became pregnant. She would lay her hands on my tummy and feel the baby move and kick. One particular night, while I was lying in bed, the baby was very active. I called Danielle in to sit by me and I placed her hand on the side of my huge tummy. Then I pushed the other side of it to start the baby moving. When I did that, the baby kicked its foot up by my ribs. We could almost feel the whole footprint through my skin. Danielle insisted on doing it over and over again because she was so amazed. She found so much joy in my pregnancy that she helped me enjoy it, too.

On November 30, 1998, Cole, our son, was born. I made sure that Danielle was one of the first to hold him. She was so proud. She wore a t-shirt that said "I'm the big sister." At home she took on the duties of being a "mini-mom." She loved feeding and rocking him as well as helping to bathe him. My nervousness about there being ten years difference in their ages vanished quickly.

Cole was only five months old when Mark and I purchased our first home. It was an older house, but we loved it because it was <u>ours</u>. The house had a large fenced-in backyard and was ideal for a family with children. Upstairs there were two bedrooms. Danielle took the larger one and decorated it with posters and "girlie" things. Cole used the smaller upstairs bedroom and Mark and I slept in the third one which was on the first floor.

While I was growing up I always knew that I would have two children—a girl and a boy. So, at that point, with my husband, Mark, and my children, Danielle and Cole, I felt that my family was complete. However, God had a different plan for me. When Cole was six months old and we had been in our new home for only a month, I learned that I was expecting again. That news was just a little shocking, coming as it did so soon after the other pregnancy, but God has His own plan and His own way.

Danielle was just as happy and excited about our having this baby as she had been about Cole's birth, but she did comment, "Mom, this had better be my little sister." I had to laugh at that and replied, "Well, we can't just order what we want, Boo." As luck would have it, she got her wish. On March 10, 2000, her little sister, Casey, joined our happy family.

She had all kinds of ideas for a baby sister, things she couldn't do with a brother. She wanted to put bows in Casey's hair and put on the cutest little outfits we could find. She wanted to teach her how to put on make-up and nail polish. I said, "Slow down honey, you have to wait until she grows up."

Everything seemed perfect.

Chapter 2

"Quiet Before The Storm"

One day Danielle came home from school with a very large bruise on her arm. It covered an area from the middle of her forearm to the middle of her upper arm. The bruise looked as though she had had blood drawn and the puncture had continued to bleed under the skin. I immediately asked her, "How did you get that?" She couldn't remember for sure but offered this explanation, "I think someone dropped a book at school and it hit my arm." I was unconvinced that just being hit by a dropped book could cause such a large bruise.

To add to the mystery, only a week later Danielle showed up with another bruise. That one was on the back of her arm all the way from the elbow to the armpit. Not only was I mystified, but I was perturbed as well when I asked, "Where did that come from?" She answered, "I was playing at my friend's house and fell backward into a chair." Then I scolded her, "Danielle, you cannot play so rough. You are hurting yourself badly!"

Soon after that I made an appointment with the pediatrician for Casey, the baby, to have her two-month shots. I have a lot of trust in the doctor so, while talking to the receptionist; I asked if he would have time to take a look at Danielle's bruising during the same appointment. She said, "Yes, come right after lunch." I still remember the exact date; it was May 16, 2000.

We waited only a little while after arriving at the office before being ushered into an examining room. The doctor appeared shortly and then gave Casey her check-up and her shots.

After he was finished with Casey, the doctor turned his full focus on Danielle. He looked at the bruise, asked a couple of questions and then told her to undress because he wanted to see her legs. When he had examined them, he turned to me and asked, "Do you see these?" He pointed to tiny red dots on her skin. "Yes." I replied. "Your daughter's blood is not clotting as it should and it is showing up as these small dots called petechiae." he added. Then he went on to explain that her CBC (complete blood count) probably was not normal and the cause could be anything from a blood infection to leukemia.

The doctor asked me to take Danielle to the laboratory for a blood test. He wrote STAT on the order because he wanted it done right away. When we got there, both of us were a bit nervous because Danielle had never before had blood drawn. As calmly as I could, I explained that she would feel a "pick" of the needle but it would not be very painful. During the procedure, Danielle was very brave and didn't even flinch.

It was about a half hour's drive home from the laboratory and by the time we reached there I had myself convinced we probably wouldn't receive the results from the test for a couple of days. I assumed it was just an infection that could be cleared up by a prescription. It would be simple—nothing bad—because bad things only happen to other people.

The phone rang just as we walked in the house. It was the doctor's office and the doctor, himself, was making the call. "This is strange," I mused, "I would have thought that the nurse would do the calling to let us know that it was an infection." The doctor's tone was very serious. He explained that the blood tests showed Danielle's blood count was dangerously low. He was surprised that she was not feeling sicker than she was. Then he announced, "I have arranged for a bed at Hurley Hospital and she needs to go there now!"

As the doctor was talking to me I thought, "He must be wrong. Look at her. Danielle is a normal, healthy child except for one large bruise. No! I know that labs can make mistakes and this is a mistake." I agreed to take her to the hospital because someone, somewhere, needed to straighten this out. The doctor's last words on the phone, "She has either aplastic anemia or leukemia" scared me but I was convinced that it would not take long to learn what really was wrong with her.

I called my sister and explained what was happening with Danielle. The news stunned her. She offered to take care of Cole and Casey and said that she also would call my mom and some of the churches in our area in order to start a prayer line.

Hurley Hospital was a forty-five minute drive from our house and, because I was not sure of the way, Mark said that he would take us there. During the ride we were very quiet. I don't think that we knew what to say to one another. I was in the front passenger seat and Danielle was right behind me. I remember once when I turned around to look at her, she began to cry. I reached back and put my hand on hers and said, "Boo, no matter what it is that you have, or whatever you have to go through, I will never leave you. I will always be right by your side." She nodded her head and I turned to look out the front window of the car.

As we rode toward the hospital I had a mixture of thoughts. I knew that leukemia was a type of cancer but had no idea what aplastic anemia was. I didn't want Danielle to have cancer so I prayed to God, "Please let it be aplastic anemia." Was I starting to actually accept the

7

idea that this is something more serious? Everything seemed so unreal that I thought, "This is just a horrible dream and I'll wake up soon." The drive seemed to go on forever.

What would they do at the hospital?

Chapter 3

Our Lives Become Chaotic

When we reached the hospital, we left the car in the parking ramp and took the elevator to the main floor. Unsure of where we were supposed to go first, we walked down a long hallway that was lined with pictures. On either side we saw doors leading to specialists' offices. I remember the sweet bitter smell of medicines and cleaning solvents hitting us in the face.

We walked up to the front desk and a lady asked "could I help you?" I answered, "Yes, my daughter is suppose to be admitted, but we're not sure what we're suppose to do from here". She pointed us in the direction of admitting so we could fill out paper work. When that was taken care of we were escorted to the 2nd floor the pediatric floor.

This unit is set up with two doors separated by a very wide wall. Those doors are locked at all times. In order to visit a child who is a patient there, you have to use the phone mounted on the wall to the right next to a camera. After you call the nurse's desk she will buzz to "unlock" the door and it will open. I liked the fact that not just anyone could visit the children in the unit.

Just after we had Danielle settled in her room, a parade of doctors and interns began coming in one after another. All of them seemed to be asking the same questions and doing the same checkups on Danielle. When that had gone on for a while, I started losing my patience. I wanted some answers and soon!

At last two doctors came in and asked to talk with me. When they introduced themselves I learned that the first, an older man, was named Dr. Inoue, the second was a woman I will call Dr. "O." (She has a long last name that is very hard to spell so we'll stick with Dr. O.) They both were very nice and seemed to understand our concern. Sometimes it must be hard for doctors to be understanding and have patience with the parents of each child that comes in. I imagine that they would rather go straight to work because they know what must be done.

The two doctors explained to us that Danielle had to have a bone marrow biopsy in order for them to know exactly what was going on. They said that the marrow would be taken from the hip bone through the back. After numbing an area on Danielle's back, they would then insert a hollow needle, cut away a small fragment of bone, and draw up some of the marrow. Later the sample of marrow would be examined under a microscope. They warned us that the procedure could be painful.

The doctors gave me a choice of stepping out of the room or staying there during the procedure. I had made a promise to Danielle I was going to stay. She was given Benadryl which made her very sleepy and everything seemed to be going well. I tried to watch what they were doing but couldn't see much except for an instrument being exchanged between hands. I <u>was</u> able to see when they drew the marrow into a syringe. The cutting of the bone and the drawing up of the marrow was the painful part for Danielle because all of a sudden her grip tightened on my hand. In order to take her mind from the ordeal, I talked to her about anything I could think of. When the procedure was finished, that was when I came to the realization that this whole thing <u>was</u> happening. It was not just a laboratory mistake and not a dream.

We were both frightened. Except for the happy time when Danielle was born, that was the first stay in a hospital for either of us. Danielle had a private bathroom in her room so I locked myself in there because I didn't want her to see how upset I was. I sat down on the floor and began to cry. A few moments later a nurse knocked on the door to ask if I was all right. I answered, "Yes." but I really wanted to scream, "NO!" They just didn't seem to understand. This very morning I had a normal eleven year old daughter and now doctors were telling me she is very sick. She doesn't look or act sick. I just had to watch my daughter go through something I had never heard of before. No, I'm not okay! I'm sitting on the floor of a hospital bathroom crying, trying to understand, and wondering what in the world I'm going to say to Danielle when I come out!

Finally, I got up, wet a towel with cold water and washed my face. I couldn't let her see that I was so scared I was crying. She was only going to be able to stay together because of my strength. I had to tell her everything was going to be okay. I took a deep breath, opened the door and walked over to Danielle's bed and said, "Are you okay, Boo?" She looked at me and answered, "Yes." I know she had to be just as scared as I was, but, she was putting on a brave front too.

This is very real. It is not a dream.

Chapter 4

An Attempt At Treatment

Danielle was diagnosed with severe aplastic anemia. The doctors explained that her bone marrow was not producing blood cells. At the time I was glad it was not leukemia. I was to soon learn that, of the two, leukemia has a much better cure rate and a standard, "by the book" treatment; aplastic anemia does not. Aplastic anemia is rare, has an unknown cause and no standard treatment for it.

When I left the hospital, Danielle was resting comfortably. They had given her an IV to transfuse whole blood and platelets in order to raise her complete blood count (CBC). I went home to see the babies; but, also, I wanted to read everything I could find on the internet about aplastic anemia.

Some of what I read I didn't believe. One article stated, "Most patients die within eighteen to twenty-four months after being diagnosed". I learned about various therapies and treatments for the disease and wondered which would be the right cure for Danielle. One of the treatments discussed in the articles was a bone marrow transplant. I read about several of the various doctors who had treated aplastic anemia. One of them wrote about a "clinical trial" that he was conducting. I knew that a trial is <u>only</u> an experiment in medicine. Eventually my eyes went blurry from all the reading.

The next day after returning to the hospital, the doctors met with us and explained what they would like to do. First, our immediate family (Cole, Casey and I) were to be tested to see if we would be compatible donors for a bone marrow transplant. They said that it was highly unlikely that any of us would be a match, but it was definitely worth a try. Then they said that they had decided on Danielle's first type of treatment. It was a procedure that went by the initials ATG.

ATG is an immunosuppressive drug therapy. The drug used is a horse-based serum, which means that the material is first injected into a horse and then extracted again. The treatment, if successful, would suppress Danielle's immune system and allow her bone marrow to grow back. The serum hangs from an IV pole and is infused over a period of six to eight hours.

"There is a high rate of allergic reaction and one of those could be anaphylactic shock." Dr. Inoue warned.

Apparently I wasn't listening to him because I wasn't nervous. I thought that sort of reaction was rare and, after all, we <u>are</u> in a hospital. To me the treatment sounded less scary than the biopsy she had already been through.

Before they could begin the treatment, they had to do a test area on Danielle. A nurse used a syringe to inject some ATG serum just under the skin on the inside of her arm. Then she sat with her for an hour. Every fifteen minutes she recorded what the injection site looked like. When the hour had passed the spot was a little red, but otherwise Danielle seemed to be having no problems. Dr. Inoue decided to go on with the treatment.

The nurse connected the IV to a machine that controlled the rate at which the serum was to be infused. She needed to stay in the room until the first few drops entered Danielle's body. I sat on one side of the bed and the nurse on the other. Very slowly one drip went in and then another. At that moment, Danielle complained, "Mom, my stomach doesn't feel good!" As soon as she ended that sentence, she sat upright in bed and tried to say "I can't breathe!" as she gasped for air.

The nurse, reaching up to touch Danielle, said, "Are you okay?"

"No!" I screamed, "She just told you she couldn't breathe!"

The nurse stopped the machine as I ran out into the hall and yelled to the doctor. "We need help! The treatment just started and Danielle can't breathe!"

Once I had said that and actually heard the words leave my lips, I went into a panic. I'm not sure how many there were, but a lot of doctors and nurses ran by me into Danielle's room. I just couldn't go back in there yet. I didn't want to see what they were going to do to her if it was really serious. In the hallway I sat on a stool and wept. A nurse walked by and asked if I was okay. I nodded my head "Yes" but I was really scared.

After a while Dr. Inoue came out of Danielle's room and said, "She's okay. She had a reaction to the ATG."

I went back into Danielle's room; she grabbed me and said, "Mom, I thought I was going to die. I was so scared!" As I hugged her tightly, I glanced at the machine. Only four drops had gone into Danielle's bloodstream, but those four little drops were going to cause her still more problems. As time went by, her lips started to swell and her blood pressure plummeted. When I asked the nurse what caused that, she said that it was another reaction to the medicine.

That night I slept with Danielle in her room. It was nice, but funny, too. It makes me laugh now when I think about how frustrating it was for the two of us to fit together in that narrow hospital bed. To take my mind off the seriousness of the situation, I tried to picture us on an outing. I imagined we were in a hotel of some sort, doing "girl things" together. I guess that sometimes it helps a little when you play tricks on your mind and daydream of something better.

The next morning, though, the reality of the situation returned when I happened to catch a glimpse of Danielle's arm where the pre-test had been done. It was badly discolored and swollen. Plus, there was a red line going up her arm away from the puncture point. I thought to myself, "If only they had waited a bit longer than an hour on the pre-test, they might have foreseen a reaction of that sort coming."

During his rounds that morning, Dr. Inoue explained, "Danielle couldn't take the ATG procedure. I'm not sure what treatment we're going to try next; so, for now, she can go home."

My reaction was, "Yes! Danielle is coming home! She is fine. Everything is going to be okay now." I was still in denial.

The doctor qualified his permission for her to go home by indicating that there would be certain rules that had to be followed. First, she would have to come back to the hospital clinic every other day for blood drawing in order to check on her complete blood count (CBC). If that was acceptable for another day, she could go home. If it was too low, she had to stay for a transfusion of whole blood and/or platelets. Second, she would not be allowed to be in large crowds or with anyone who was ill. Danielle's immune system was too weak to fight off germs that she might pick up. Third, she would be unable to finish the rest of the school year or to continue in her church group. Danielle was not very happy about that because she loved both of those activities.

Danielle still had another hurdle to overcome before she could be checked out of the hospital. The doctors suggested that they surgically implant a port, which is a permanent IV line into her body. There are two kinds of ports that are most often used with children. The first is surgically attached to a major vein or artery inside the chest wall and has one end hanging out a small incision near the breast bone. The second is a circular port under the skin near the clavicle bone. It, too, is attached to a vein or artery but does not protrude from the body. Because it lies under the skin, the patient can bathe and swim without concern over keeping it dry or it's becoming infected. We chose the second type.

The thought of having surgery to place the port made Danielle nervous, but the nurses administered something to relax her before she went in. It made her a little giggly, which was a small blessing. When she came out of the operating room, the doctors had accessed the port (opened it up). Seeing something sticking out of her skin looked very strange to me.

Later, we found that it was very nice having the port so that Danielle did not need to have her arm continually picked for IVs. When she did need an IV, they just used an "L" shaped needle for puncturing the skin over the small circle of the port. Each time the port was used, it was vital that it be flushed with a saline solution to keep it clean and then with heparin to prevent clotting. They gave me a white crème called Emla. Before going to the clinic, I was supposed to put it on the port area and then place a place a plastic cover over it. The crème numbed the area to be poked.

Once, when I knew that they would have to access the port, I forgot put the crème on the circle ahead of time. I was very upset and apologized to Danielle saying, "Boo, I'm so sorry!"

"Mom, that's okay, it only stings a little." was her brave reply.

"No, it's not okay, Boo. You've gone through so much and if I can save you from even one little sting or one more little pain, then I should always remember to do it!," I said.

One failed treatment, how many other choices do we have now?

Chapter 5

Commuting From Home

For about a month and a half we traveled back and forth every other day from Vassar to the hospital for Danielle's checkups. We trudged through the long hallways, took the elevator to the upper floor where we were met by the same two nurses. They drew the samples of blood which would determine whether she would have to stay for a transfusion or if we could go back home that day.

Each time, as a reward when the test was finished, Danielle was allowed to select a prize from a collection in a box. During the first couple of visits, she picked out something for herself, but after that she began selecting toys that she would give to Cole and Casey. When Christmas time came around, the prize box held Christmas bears and Danielle collected six of them to give to me. She is a very giving type of person.

At home one night I was in the bedroom shared by Cole and Casey. Cole was asleep, but Casey was awake having her night bottle. Danielle came in and asked if she could cuddle up next to me on the floor with a blanket. She wanted to watch television while I fed Casey. I said, "Sure, Boo." She lay there for a while and then got up and went into the bathroom. A few moments later she came out holding some toilet paper to her nose. I asked what was wrong. She said, "I have a bloody nose." That was a sign that her blood platelets were low and that she needed a transfusion.

That really bothered me because I had always thought of our home as a safe haven where everything would be okay. It would be our own sanctuary because here we could have our entire family around us providing protection. During the past few weeks we had been trying to live as normally as we could under the circumstances. For me that nosebleed was just one more example of reality slapping me in the face because I realized that I couldn't even protect Danielle in our own home.

This was my acceptance time.

Chapter 6

An Important Decision

In June, Dr. Inoue developed heart problems and had to take a leave of absence from Hurley Hospital. At the same time, Dr. O was out of the country on a trip. Those two events meant Danielle would be without a doctor. Before his leave went into effect, Dr. Inoue began making arrangements for all of his patients to be referred to doctors in other hospitals. Because I assumed that we would have a choice of where Danielle would be referred, I had already chosen the Mott Children's Hospital in Ann Arbor, but that wasn't to be the case at all.

"Danielle is being transferred to the Detroit Children's Hospital." The nurse said when she met with us.

"Could we go to Mott instead?" I asked.

She went on to explain, "All Danielle's information has already been forwarded to Detroit but, if you insist, I can talk to Dr. Inoue and possibly he can get her into the Ann Arbor hospital."

"No, that's all right." I responded. "He is really sick with heart problems and I don't want to put any more stress on him. If it is already set up in Detroit, then we'll go there."

On July 5, 2000, we found ourselves in a Detroit clinic waiting to meet the new doctor. I had already pictured the man in my mind. He would be a foreigner who would be hard to understand he would know exactly what he was doing, and he would hurriedly explain everything to me in medical terminology that I wouldn't be able to comprehend. The man who walked in was not at all what I had pictured. The doctor was stocky, balding, and quiet spoken; he had a gentle way about him. He introduced himself as Dr. Abella and he was very pleasant.

First, Dr. Abella sat with us and asked a few questions. Then he examined Danielle and seemed very willing to stay as long as we needed him. He talked about his plans for Danielle's treatment and indicated he wanted to start immediately. He explained to us that since there had been no match for her bone marrow in the United States Registry, he was putting her on the International Registry. He explained further that Danielle would need to undergo another bone marrow biopsy because he had to have his own record of her marrow. Naturally that news did not go over very well with her.

Dr. Abella told us that he wanted to attempt two different types of treatment for Danielle's condition. One of them was similar to ATG, except that it used a rabbit-based instead of a horse-based serum. The second type of treatment he planned to use was high-dose cyclophosphamide (chemotherapy). He said that we could try the rabbit-based serum (ALG) first if we decided to; but, if that didn't work, then he still wanted to use the other.

Earlier I had read about chemotherapy as a treatment for aplastic anemia still being in the clinical trial stage. It was being used mainly at Johns Hopkins Hospital in Baltimore, Maryland, and had only been tried two times in Michigan to my knowledge. The doctor explained that the treatment was experimental and consisted of four days of high dose chemo. Before Danielle could even begin the therapy, tests would have to be conducted on her heart to see if she could withstand the dosage. He also said that Danielle probably would never be able to have children of her own because she would be sterile as a result of the therapy. In addition, she would lose all her hair and be very ill for a time. The chemotherapy was intended to wipe out all of her bone marrow cells and, hopefully, in time they would grow back and be healthy again. With all the information he had given us to consider, I asked if we could go home and have the night to talk about it and make the decision. He agreed to that plan.

At home Danielle and I had our own little discussion, just the two of us. We talked and talked. I needed to know exactly how she felt about what was being offered to her from the treatment. We talked about her becoming very sick from it, about losing her hair and especially about the probability of her ending up sterile. As we discussed those very serious topics I wondered, "How can I make an eleven year old understand all this?"

When I asked Danielle if she minded not being able to have babies of her own, her answer was, "I have always wanted, someday, to adopt children anyway."

Then I told her, "Boo, if you feel that way, maybe it's because God knew that you were going to go through this chemo and probably not be able to have children, and He has already picked out a very special baby that is going to need you someday."

Danielle and I talked about everything that had to do with her body and her treatments. I wanted her to feel like she still had some control over her life. She had to know everything that was going on. The one thing that I <u>did</u> <u>not</u> tell her was that this disease could be fatal. I couldn't even think of that and I felt certain that she would beat the problem anyway. So, it was not even an issue.

The choice rested heavily on me. I knew that, no matter what, <u>my</u> decision was the final one. I would have the last say in it. After our talk, Danielle said that she wanted to go through with the chemotherapy. So, I decided to follow her wishes and said, "Okay. After all, Dr. Abella had said that if the rabbit serum didn't work, he wanted to use the chemo anyway. So, why not just skip a treatment and, instead of going through two of them, just go right to the chemo?" The decision was made.

Chapter 7

Another Attempt At Treatment

On July 6, 2000, I phoned Dr. Abella to inform him of our decision. Before telling him I asked if he had ever used chemotherapy before. He said, "Yes, once." Then there was a pause, and I just had to ask, "How did it turn out?" The doctor hesitated as he replied, "Not very well, the child was extremely sick when he finally received treatment."

That answer made it even harder for me to tell him that we had chosen the chemotherapy.

As soon as the doctor knew our decision, he wondered if we could be at the hospital the next morning.

"Wow, that fast?" I asked. I guess I wasn't expecting it to be so soon. There was much to do in a very short time. I had to pack for Danielle, for both of the babies and for myself.

My family had been telling me to leave Cole and Casey at home but there was no way that I was abandoning a twenty-month old and a four-month old for an entire week without their mom. Cole and Casey would never be able to understand why I had left them behind. Besides that, they were a big part of what made me smile each day and I really needed that at the time. When I looked at them playing or heard them laughing, my mind took a break from all the stress. They kept me going.

We arrived at the hospital on the morning of the seventh and learned that a full day had been planned for us. First, the doctor's assistant was going to do a bone marrow biopsy. It was to be Danielle's second one, so she knew what to expect but that didn't make it any less painful. Fortunately the assistant was very good at the procedure and also fast. Those, together, were little blessings.

I had started looking for little blessings in everyday things: the biopsy being fast, having a hospital room all to ourselves where we could do whatever we wanted, or being able to order anything we wished from the hospital menu—all little things, but they did add up.

Next, Danielle had to have a catheter inserted through which the chemo would escape. Because the medicine was very, very strong, it could not stay in her body and needed a direct path out of it. I prepared her as well as I could by explaining exactly what a catheter was and why it was necessary. Danielle was able to accept all of that and seemed to be okay with it. Then came a shock for both of us.

When the nurse walked in with the catheter, he turned out to be a male!

I thought, "What could be worse? My eleven-year old daughter will have an adult male touching her private parts! As I left the room I wondered, "What is <u>Danielle</u> thinking? She's at a weird stage in her life, just starting puberty, and she's probably really embarrassed. I know I would be. Couldn't the hospital have let a female nurse do the catheterization?"

Somehow we both made it over that hurdle.

Danielle was to receive four days of chemotherapy. When she had been given her pre-meds, the first bag was hung on the IV pole and it began to drip. We were both tense but I was on the edge of my seat with fear and anticipation. The first few drops went in. Nothing happened. "So far, so good." I thought. In a few moments both of us began to relax a little because some of the medicine was already in her body and there seemed to be no reaction. Later on in the evening, Danielle started getting a headache but the nurse gave her a medication for it. She also had to have an infusion of blood platelets.

That night the babies and I checked into the Ronald McDonald House located immediately in front of the hospital. Before leaving, I told Danielle, "We are going to our room for the night, but we're staying nearby and I'll call you before I go to bed." When we got to the R.M. House we found that it was very nice. Our room was in the basement level. It had two beds and shared a bathroom with only one other room. Upstairs, on the first floor, was the main public area which was shared by everyone. It had a living room, a kitchen and a big play area for children. It was just like a very large home. The Ronald McDonald Charities kept some food in the cupboards in case the residents were unable to shop for themselves, and, various groups and organizations came in throughout the week with a catered dinner for everyone.

It had been an emotional day for me and I decided to try to get some sleep. Before going to bed I called Danielle on the free direct line linked to the hospital. I was really expecting to get bad news or to hear that she was in misery, but I was pleasantly surprised when she answered the phone with, "Hi, Mommy." She was in a good mood.

I asked, "What are you doing?"

"Putting my clothes from my suitcase into the drawers." she said and then went on to add, "I know we picked the right treatment, Mom. I can feel it. I feel so good right now. I know this is going to work."

After we hung up I prayed to God and asked Him to be with Danielle.

The next morning I went to Danielle's room to see how she was doing. Already the chemo was taking its toll on her body and was making her very sick. She was having stomach pains, nausea and a bad headache. Thankfully, the nurses were able to give her something for the pain. In the afternoon they checked her complete blood count. That procedure had become a daily ritual in order to see whether or not she needed a transfusion. Next, they ran an EKG on Danielle before she received her next treatment of chemo. The EKG would tell them how well her heart was reacting to the massive dosage in therapy. That night and on into the next morning her heart remained strong.

On the final day of the chemotherapy, I said to Danielle, "If only you can get through this last dose then you'll start to feel better. Just hold on the best you can." I started singing the chorus of "Hold on for one more Day" by Wilson Phillips. Soon Danielle began to sing with me. From then on it became "our song."

Although the nurses gave her attavan and morphine for her stomach pains and headaches, Danielle continued to moan in agony. It was very hard to listen to her. I tried to think of <u>anything</u> that would make her smile—even if it was only a little smile.

"Boo," I laughed, "if you keep moaning like that because of your stomach, then we'll put you in the Labor and Delivery unit so that you will have someone else to moan along with."

I think that sometimes you try too hard to find comforting words to say and then when you do think of something, it sounds terrible as soon as it leaves your mouth. Surprisingly, that seemed to work because she did smile for a second. The nurse gave Danielle more medicine which appeared to ease the pain a little but she was still sick to her stomach.

I remember thinking to myself as I watched her enduring all that torture, "She is so strong! She is stronger than most of the adults I know. Here she is, only eleven years old, battling a terrible disease but acting as though everything is okay. <u>I have a really awesome daughter.</u>" When she talks it is never about herself, but always about others. She hardly ever complains and can still smile. Before her diagnosis when I looked at Danielle, I just saw my little girl. But now I can see that she has grown up during the past few weeks, right before my eyes. She seems very grown up and yet very fragile at the same time.

That night while lying in bed at the Ronald McDonald House, I prayed, "Please, God, touch Danielle's ovaries and uterus. Cover them in protection so that she doesn't lose that part of herself." I asked God to carry out <u>His</u> will, and if she wasn't able to have her own babies, then to please make certain that she finds the most special, caring, and "just meant for her" baby in the whole world.

I lay there picturing what it would be like when Danielle grew up and was married. I thought of her crying because she wanted children but couldn't have them. That really hurt because I was helpless and unable to protect her from that possibility. However, I shook off the thought and said to myself, "We'll just have to deal with that when it comes and ask God to help us."

I have noticed that people around Danielle and me react to her being ill in different ways. Throughout these past few weeks my sister, Alisha, has become my rock. I lean on her continually for support and can call on her night and day. She willingly takes care of Cole and Casey on only a second's notice whenever I need her. I only hope that someday she can fully understand all that she has done for me during this crisis.

My husband, Mark, is trying to be supportive of both Danielle and me, but the stress is beginning to get to him. I am hardly ever at home any more and my entire world revolves around Danielle. At one point he said to me, "I just don't know if I can handle this." He was even thinking about leaving me; and who could blame him? The disease has taken a toll on our new marriage but will not break it. The marriage started with a strong foundation and I know in my heart that we will overcome. Our union will end up even stronger because we have endured this.

It is probably a good thing that we can't see into the future.

Chapter 8

Frustration Turns To Anger

Everything seemed to be ganging up on me. I was becoming overly stressed and very homesick. I just wanted so badly to go home for at least one night in order to get my bearings once again, but I couldn't leave Danielle there by herself. Even though I wasn't inside the hospital all the time, she knew I was close by in the Ronald McDonald House. Staying in Detroit began to wear on me, too. The hospital was in a bad part of the city and I had to make sure that I was back at the R. M. House by 5:00 p.m. because I didn't feel safe walking from the hospital to the house after dark.

I was beginning to lose faith in the hospital staff as well. One time Danielle asked for chocolate milk and the nurses never brought it to her. A few nights later she felt very cold and asked if she could have an extra blanket. They didn't bring it either.

When I called her that night from the R. M. House to talk and wish her good night, she mentioned the blanket and also said, "Mom, I'm hungry."

"Well, what did you have for dinner? I asked.

Her answer stunned me. "Nothing. They didn't bring me a dinner tray."

After hearing that, I reached the boiling point. I grabbed Cole and Casey and we marched back to the hospital and up to Danielle's room. She <u>still</u> had not had dinner or been given a blanket. I ran out in the hallway to the linen storage and started looking for something to cover her. A nurse finally noticed me there and asked what I was doing. I said,

"A few nights ago my daughter asked for chocolate milk and didn't get it. Now she is cold and asked for a blanket which she didn't get. And, while I'm at it, she hasn't had dinner yet either! She is not a new admit her dinner tray should have been here," I told her. The nurse acted surprised and had no answers for me. She offered to get Danielle a sandwich and something to go with it.

I yelled, "A sandwich, for <u>dinner</u>?" It didn't make me happy, but it was better than nothing, so I decided to hold my tongue.

The day after Danielle ended her final chemo treatment; the doctors released her to my care but insisted that we stay on the hospital grounds at the Ronald McDonald House. I agreed. That night I took all three of them to the house and we settled into our room. By the time I had the kids tucked in, it was probably ten or eleven o'clock and I went to bed. I lay there wide awake. I just couldn't get to sleep. All of a sudden I went into a panic attack. I got out of bed, dressed and brought the car around to the front door. I packed our bags, loaded up the children and headed for home. I felt better as soon as we turned onto the freeway because I was homebound and all the children were with me.

About a half hour into the two-hour drive home, I reached over and felt Danielle's forehead. She was burning up with fever.

"We have to go back." I told her.

She began crying and begged, "No, Mommy, no! I don't want to go back there!"

It would be impossible for her to go home now, but what was I supposed to do? I knew she had to go back to the hospital, but how could I break her heart after all she had gone through? Then I decided what to do. I told her, "I'll go the rest of the way home so you can get a little break. But, after we get there, Mark will drive you to Detroit again." She seemed to accept that and we enjoyed the rest of the trip home.

When we got there, she was upset all over again about not being able to stay home. I took her temperature and it was 103°. Then I felt guilt for having taken her so far away from the hospital. I asked Mark to drive her back to Detroit. I just couldn't do it because I needed sleep and just a little peace of mind away from that place. I told him, "Take her down there and tell the doctors that you are going home immediately so that I can go in the morning and be with her."

Early the next morning I was again on my way to the hospital. The doctors ran blood cultures to see if Danielle had an infection causing the high fever. Those tests came back negative. That was a good sign and meant that the probable cause was her low white blood count resulting from the chemotherapy.

On July 16, Danielle was able to come home from the hospital. Once again there was a restriction. She had to wear a mask to prevent her breathing in anything that might make her sick. Her white blood cells, which usually protect a person against germs, were in short supply due to the chemo treatment. That meant that she was vulnerable to anything that was in the air.

Only a couple of days later we found ourselves once more on our way to Detroit because of Danielle's rising fever. When we left home it was 102°, by the time we checked her into the hospital, it had risen to

103°. On our way in I took a moment to talk to the doctor. She said that they weren't particularly concerned with how high the temperature was but, instead, what it was doing to her internally.

As soon as I got to Danielle's room, I took her temperature again. It had risen to 103.5°. Fifteen minutes passed and still no one came to her room. The next time I checked, her temperature was at 104° and we had been at the hospital for over half an hour. All my frustrations about that hospital began to build up in me and I furiously stomped out of the room. Just outside I stopped the doctor in her tracks. I raised my voice and demanded that Danielle be seen now! I screamed, "If you are so worried about what this fever is doing to her internally, then why hasn't anyone seen her yet? In just a half hour her temperature has risen to 104°!"

While I was at it, I released all my anger over how Danielle was being treated (or mistreated) at that hospital. I told the doctor that I no longer trusted leaving my daughter in their care, and if I could move her to another hospital, I would do it in a second. I was yelling by the time I was done "explaining" everything to that doctor. Everyone in the vicinity of where we were heard it all. All my anger and frustration and loneliness were taken out in that hallway. I was starting to feel like this was mine and Danielle's battle. It wasn't just hers alone.

In thinking that way, I started to isolate myself from other people. I didn't have time to share my feelings with anyone. I didn't have as much contact with my family and I kept a lot of things to myself. Once, when Danielle was first diagnosed, I left her at the hospital and went to my sisters to pick up the babies. When I arrived there, I just sat on her floor and cried. I just kept saying, "I don't know how she got so sick." Other than that I didn't break down in front of people too often.

Instead of getting rid of my anger, I was feeding it.

Chapter 9

God Is Listening

We are still traveling for her CBC and transfusions when she needs them. The doctors are watching her counts very closely right now. I also am very active in knowing what is going on with Danielle. Every visit I receive a print out of all her counts. I'm starting to get a stack of papers gathered.

It's like being on pins and needles. Her fever still goes up and down. On July twenty-first, her fever went very high, when we checked into Hurley Hospital it was 105. They transported Danielle by ambulance back to Detroit Children's to try and control it. She wanted to stay at Hurley so badly, but the two doctors had not yet returned. She was attached to the nurses at Hurley and felt more comfortable there.

In Detroit the doctors ran all the tests again for any kind of infection, they came back negative. I decided to come home that night. It was about 9 p.m. when I started driving. Worried about leaving Danielle at the hospital, I started to pray. I was praying, "God touch Danielle and keep her close tonight." I told Him I just couldn't be there; I needed to go home to my "safe haven" just for a while.

I went into a daze while I was praying and saw Danielle lying on the hospital bed. She didn't have a sheet on, just the hospital gown. She looked like she was asleep, peacefully. Then she just very gently rose about a foot off the bed. There was nothing between the bed and her. It looked as though I could see right under her. But I knew what it was, it was God's hand. I felt it. It was huge; it lay beneath the whole length of her body and caressed her. It looked like she fit there in the palm of His hand perfectly, she belonged there. Right then I felt peace; I've never felt that close to God before in prayer.

I looked at the clock and it said 10 p.m. I still have another hour to go before I get home. I hadn't remembered the last few minutes of the drive. Quite sometime had passed and I have no recollection of it, except my vision.

As soon as I walked in the door of home, I called the hospital. I couldn't talk to Danielle because the phone doesn't ring into the rooms past 10 p.m., but I could talk to her nurse. I asked, "How is she doing?"

The nurse answered, "Good, her fever broke about 10 o'clock and she is sleeping now."

I was very relieved, "Thank you God for my answer."

I have, even if just for a little while, a sense of peace.

Chapter 10

An Imperfect Picture

Knowing that Danielle probably would lose her hair because of the chemotherapy, I decided to take all the children to the Kmart Portrait Studio and have their pictures taken. On the day we chose to go there, Danielle was tired but said she felt well enough for that.

At the studio there were two women in charge. Both of them came inside the prop room with us. Danielle excitedly told them that she had money in her purse. She added that she had gone through chemotherapy and that people, when they visited her in the hospital, had given it to her so that she could look forward to going shopping after coming home again. I explained that the reason we were there was that I wanted pictures taken in case she lost her hair.

One of the women lifted the children up on a table to have them pose and Danielle put the purse by her side. After a couple different shots had been taken, they were told to move their positions into different poses before more were taken. Then I asked Danielle, "Where is your purse?" She looked all around the area near her but it was gone. We searched through everything. I even looked all along the length of the store aisle leading to the studio. I knew I wasn't going to find it there, because Danielle had the purse next to her on the table.

I was sure that one of the two women in the studio had taken the purse but couldn't prove it. We went to the customer service desk at the front of the store and reported it missing. A lady there made the announcement and gave a description of the purse over the loudspeaker. She said that if anyone found it to please bring it to the front of the store.

Danielle and I looked at one another and both of us were in tears. I thought to myself, "That money was hers as a result of being sick. The lady knew that, so how could she take it from her?" I was furious and wanted to call the police immediately and have the two women searched until we found the purse. Danielle sat down on the floor by the customer service desk. I could tell that she was terribly disappointed and besides that she wasn't feeling well either. She needed to be taken home right away.

Later that day I called the Kmart store and talked to the people in charge. They refused to do anything about the lost purse and didn't even offer to replace the money in it. Sometimes people can be so unfeeling. To make her feel better, I told Danielle that I would try to make up the money she had lost.

Chapter 11

Surprises

Nine days after Danielle finished with the chemotherapy, she still had all her hair but there were some other problems that needed solving. At that time the two main difficulties seemed to be her lack of appetite and her frequent high fevers. I had a hard time finding something—anything—that she would even take one bite of. Consequently she was losing weight. The doctors felt that they had to bring the high fevers under control before they could decide which treatment to try next. Everyone watched her blood counts very carefully.

I became almost obsessed with each detail connected with Danielle's illness. At the hospital I wanted to know everything that was going on so I asked questions constantly. Each night at home I turned on the computer and looked for whatever information I could find on the subject. It was almost the only thing I thought of all day long.

Many nights I did not stay overnight at the hospital because I needed breaks from the place. If Danielle had something important to go through the next day, I did stay with her. Usually I had Cole and Casey with me and I couldn't see how all four of us could sleep in Danielle's narrow bed. So, I went home most nights. Then the first thing the next morning, I packed up our necessities, drove to the hospital and spent most of the day with her.

On July 22, fifteen days after the chemotherapy was completed, I called Danielle to tell her that I was just leaving home and would be there in a couple of hours. Later, when I walked into her room, for a moment I thought that I had the wrong one. A stranger, who was completely bald, was in Danielle's bed! She rolled over and said, "Hi Mom." I was speechless! My mouth dropped open and I just stared at her for a minute.

"Boo, how come you didn't tell me when I called this morning?" was all I could sputter.

"I wanted to surprise you." she giggled.

Wow! Danielle had lost every single strand of hair in just one night! I had expected it to come out slowly but I was completely wrong. She said that during the middle of the night, her scalp felt itchy and each time she scratched her head a clump of hair fell out in her hand. I found myself spending the whole day just looking at her and trying to get used to her new look.

That night after driving home, I called my mom. "Grab your hair-cutting kit and get over here," I said. All my life I have had very long hair and now it was down to the middle of my back. When Mom arrived I exclaimed, "Start cutting before I lose my nerve." When she was finished it was so short it didn't touch the collar of my shirt. Looking at the result in the mirror, I thought, "Hah! Now I have a surprise for Danielle." I couldn't wait to get to the hospital the next morning.

When I walked into Danielle's room the next day, she exclaimed, "No! Mom, how could you?"

"Boo," I said, "We both used to have long hair, you don't have to go through this alone. We'll grow our hair out again together."

She was fine with that. Before undergoing the chemotherapy, Danielle's hair was very straight. Once she knew that there was a good possibility she would lose her hair, she made a wish that when it came in again that it would be curly.

In a short time we had yet another nice surprise. Hurley Hospital informed us that Danielle's doctors had both returned from their leaves of absence. With Dr. Inoue and Dr. O on hand once more, Danielle could go there again for her treatment. She liked the hospital and the nurses there went out of their way to spoil her. I was relieved too, because I had great trust in the staff at Hurley Hospital and was pleased that we would be returning to it.

Chapter 12

A Happy Event

My younger sister, Alisha, became engaged and asked if Danielle could be in her wedding party as the flower girl. At the time I wasn't sure that she could even go to the celebration because there would be a large crowd of people there. I checked with the doctor who informed me that no, she would not be allowed to take part in the ceremony but yes, she could attend. It hurt me that she could not serve as the flower girl, but at least she would be able to go to it. That was still another of the small blessings I had begun keeping track of.

Alisha was upset that Danielle couldn't be in her wedding. She wondered what the difference would be between her standing during the ceremony and sitting in a pew while it went on. I explained as well as I could by saying, "Danielle couldn't go to the store for the dress fittings and she would be unable to go through the rehearsals. Also she may not have the strength to withstand all the hustle and bustle of a big wedding." We tried to make the best of the situation by being grateful that at least she could be there for the happy event.

On August 3rd, Danielle was allowed to leave the hospital. Because Cole, Casey and I were all sick with colds, she was not permitted to

40

stay at our house. For the time being, she went to my mom's home. She still continued to have frequent high fevers and because of those we often had to drive her back and forth to the clinic at Hurley. We were thankful that at least she was out of the hospital and was once again staying in Vassar.

The wedding took place just nine days later on August 12th. Danielle wore a very pretty purple dress. That color had always been her favorite. To protect her from dangerous germs she wore a face mask; to cover her bare head, she wore a du-rag. At the church we sat in a pew together as a family for the ceremony. I was happy and proud to have Danielle with us. Afterwards a photographer took pictures and then we went to a catering hall for dinner and dancing.

There was one small problem in the otherwise perfect day. As soon as we arrived I checked Danielle's temperature. It showed that she had developed another high fever. She was very disappointed and begged to be allowed to stay for the festivities and to put off going to the hospital until they were over with. I called the hospital and talked to Dr. O. She asked, "How is Danielle feeling with the fever?" I indicated that she seemed to be doing well. Then the doctor told me to give her two Tylenol tablets, watch her temperature closely and let her stay at the party. She said that I could bring her back to the clinic the next day. That made Danielle very happy and I was relieved as well. It was one more indication that the doctors at Hurley Hospital were very understanding. That was still one more small blessing.

While we were at the hall, I couldn't help but wonder how she was feeling. Is she comfortable with the fact that she will be bald for a time and that she has to wear a mask when she is in a crowd of people?

Later I learned the answers to my questions. Danielle was okay with all of it. She had a lot of fun out on the dance floor and eventually took off the du-rag and displayed her bare head. Though her face was pale and very thin, and her eyes had dark circles around them she was very beautiful to me. I loved her very much for the genuine person that she was.

Chapter 13

A Second Opinion

When Danielle had been on the International Bone Marrow Registry for two weeks, the doctor had some news for us. "Three possible matches have been found but they are not very good ones." Then he went on to say, "There are six categories that may match with one another. We want a five out of six match in order to transplant. But with those three donors Danielle is only matching four out of the six." Because of that, the decision was made to wait a little longer for a better match.

Because the bone marrow transplant would be delayed, I decided to do some more research on my own. As a part of that research, I read a report of a clinical trial using chemotherapy that was written by Doctors Robert Brodsky and Richard Jones at the Johns Hopkins Oncology Center in Baltimore, Maryland. It explained in detail about the procedures and protocols (records of treatments) that were used in the chemotherapy trial.

I obtained a copy of the trial report and from it learned this: The patients were given high dosages of cyclophosphamide (the same drug that Danielle had received at the Detroit hospital) and that was followed by injections ten days later of another drug called G-CSF (the clinical name for neupogen). Neupogen boosts the growth of white blood cells in the bone marrow. The report went on to state that it could take up to ninety-five days after the chemotherapy before there would be any signs of bone marrow recovery and re-growth. The next statement was what really impressed me about the therapy. It stated that <u>seven out of ten of the patients treated were cured of the disease!</u> I took a copy of the report to Hurley Hospital for the doctors there to read.

According to what I was able to learn, Danielle was only the second aplastic anemia patient to be treated with chemotherapy at the Detroit hospital and the first at Hurley Hospital. I decided on my own that I would make the attempt to contact the doctors who conducted the clinical trial in Baltimore. People often say that it is wise to have a second opinion and that was my wish. I had a lot of questions to ask and wanted answers for them.

Johns Hopkins is one of the best known hospitals in the United States, so naturally I was nervous about making the call. I picked up my phone and dialed the number in Baltimore. While doing that I was trying desperately to remember everything I wanted to ask about. All of a sudden I heard, "Hello. This is Dr. Brodsky." I thought, "Oh my gosh! He is actually on the phone!"

I explained about the situation with Danielle and indicated that I was concerned about what was happening with her. I mentioned that after reading his report on the clinical trials, I was interested in learning more information about them. I told him that I was most impressed with his reported success rate of seventy to eighty percent in curing the disease. After explaining everything to him and bringing him up to date on what was going on with Danielle, I asked if I could bring Danielle to Baltimore so he could treat her. His reply disappointed me. It was, "No, not at this time. The doctors in Michigan have already started the treatment there, so let them finish it. Besides, she really should not travel this far."

Dr. Brodsky did ask me to suggest that Danielle's doctors call him because he would be happy to confer with them. When I approached one of the doctors at Hurley Hospital, I got a very negative response. I explained about the success rate Dr. Brodsky had achieved with his treatment and said that he would like her to phone him so they could confer with one another. The doctor was not happy at all. She did not like the idea and sounded unwilling to contact him. I don't know if she called or not.

Chapter 14

A Birthday Celebration

Danielle managed to stay out of the hospital for a little while—that is other than for the regular clinic days—but had to be readmitted on August 13th. At the time she weighed only ninety-two pounds which contrasted sharply with the one hundred thirteen pounds that she weighed before the chemotherapy. She was extremely pale and looked much too thin. Her hair began to grow back in again but it just looked like fuzz.

The doctors kept Danielle in the hospital for the next couple of days to make certain that she had no infections. Up to that time the tests for infections had all come back negative. Even though I was thankful for the negative results, the high fever problem was awfully frustrating for me.

Danielle's birthday was going to be on August 16th and she constantly pressured the doctors about whether or not she would be able to be home for the big event. They said that she would just have to wait to see how she was doing and suggested she take it day by day. On the evening of August 15th, the night before her birthday, the doctors made the decision that she would have to remain as an in-patient for the day.

Danielle was very disappointed and looked so sad that I immediately decided that we would have a very small party for her right in her hospital room. She had the room all to herself since it was too risky for her to have another sick child sharing it with her. I went home to call some of the immediate family members and invited them to celebrate with us the following evening. That night I made signs and decorations for the party.

On the morning of the 16th, I hung the "Happy Birthday!" signs and other decorations around Danielle's room. It looked very festive and cheered our spirits while I stayed with her for a time. In the afternoon I had to run home in order to pick up the cake and the presents, as well as Cole and Casey. They, of course, were going to be a part of the celebration too. While I was gone, some of Danielle's favorite nurses went into her room to sing "Happy Birthday" and spend some of the afternoon with her. They treated her like she was their own child and it is no wonder she loved them so much.

Danielle's birthday party went as well as it could in a hospital room. She happily opened her presents and enjoyed visiting with all of the relatives who were able to attend. The party helped to take away some of the disappointment over not being able to go home. All in all she felt fairly well for the celebration.

I did notice that she had developed a cough.

Chapter 15

The Cough

Danielle was released from the hospital on August 17th, the day after her birthday. Then two days later I had to take her back again for her regular visit to the clinic to receive platelets. While she was there the nurse took her temperature and discovered that it again was high at 101.4°. If it had been only one tenth of a degree higher at 101.5°, the doctors would have kept her in the hospital. As it turned out, she was able to come home after the infusion of the platelets. Her home stay, though, was very, very short. Later that night I checked her temperature and found that it had spiked. So, back to the hospital we went and she was readmitted. Her cough seemed to be getting worse, too.

During the weeks since the chemotherapy, I had asked the doctors a couple of times about when Danielle would be given the neupogen shots which were designed to boost the white blood cells in the bone marrow and fight off infections. According to the report I had read on the clinical tests in Baltimore, the drug was to be injected ten days following the end of the chemotherapy. I felt as though the doctors were refusing to listen to me, but I was wrong. They finally ordered the shots a couple of days later. That was a great day for me even though I knew that it would probably take a while before any good results would appear.

By August 24th, Danielle seemed to be recovering from her cold because there were no bacteria in her cultures and she had not had a fever for a few days. That changed suddenly just when the doctors were talking about releasing her to go home. On the 28th her temperature went up once again. At that point they decided to try something new. Since the cultures showed negative results and she continued having fevers, they had to look elsewhere for the problem. As a result of Danielle's continuing cough, they made the decision to do an x-ray of her lungs.

The results of the x-ray were not good. They showed that Danielle had a spot of pneumonia on her right lung. Since her immune system was still seriously compromised by the chemotherapy, it was going to be necessary for her to take strong antibiotics to fight the lung infection. The doctors chose the antibiotic ampiterisan B for her treatment and they began infusing it through an IV.

Every day seemed to be the same. I was told, "No, she cannot come home yet. Yes, her blood counts continue to drop. Yes, she is being transfused." Each morning I made the trip to the hospital hoping for something to change, but usually was disappointed. In order to try to raise our spirits during that time when things seemed to be at their worst, Danielle and I often sang our song together—"Hold On For One More Day."

Two corridors down from Danielle's room in the hospital was an area that held toys, games, puzzles and other activities for children. When she was feeling well enough we would check out some of the items and work on them together in her room. Most of the time, however, she was not able to do much because the ampiterisan B made her very ill. She threw up often and just lay in bed with no energy for doing anything. A couple of times she was so weak that she couldn't get out of bed to be sick and had to throw up over the side of the bed.

Finally, there was a break in our routine. It didn't come from the doctors or nurses but from another lady who was a counselor working for the hospital. She approached Danielle and asked if she would like to be signed up with the Make A Wish Foundation. She explained that the organization would do its best to grant any wish that Danielle made. She was so excited! She decided that she wanted to go to Disney World in Florida and swim with the Dolphins. Of course, we both realized that she could not go right away, in fact, we couldn't even pick a date for it at that time. Before that happened Danielle's health would need to stabilize and she would have to be feeling better. But at least it gave us something to talk about and it was something for her to look forward to in the future.

Chapter 16

The Checkers Game

One night when Danielle was feeling particularly good, we signed out a game of checkers for us to play. It was late in the evening and I didn't have Cole and Casey with me at the time, so there were only the two of us. She and I played as we sat on the window sill in her hospital room. The furnace register was right in front of the window and it stuck out far enough to make a wide ledge.

While we were playing, we looked out at the many bright lights that were visible from our perch. Danielle's room overlooked the helipad which was two stories below and we were able to see directly down to it. That was the spot where the helicopter landed when it was delivering patients to the hospital and it was very well lighted.

Our checkers game was interrupted at one point that evening when a helicopter landed on the helipad. We watched for a few moments as it flew very near to the building before it settled on the surface of the pad. We observed as a couple of attendants carried someone from the helicopter into the hospital.

"Boo, you never want to ride in one of those," I said.

"Why?" she asked.

My reply probably scared her. "If you are riding in the hospital helicopter, then that means that you are in very bad shape and you may not live. Helicopters are only used in extremely serious emergency situations."

After the helicopter flew away, we continued with the checkers game. I remember thinking that it felt so good that the two of us were spending that girl time together. During the day the hospital is a very busy place with all sorts of activity going on constantly. At night it is much quieter and the time I spend with Danielle then is mine and mine alone.

On September 1st we got our first real ray of hope. Danielle's CBC (complete blood count) results showed that her platelets increased from 2,100 up to 2,900 completely on their own! They actually went up! Her hemoglobin count went from 8.5 up to 9.1! It, too, went up on its own! I was ecstatic. "Okay" I thought, "the treatment is starting to work. The chemotherapy must be helping Danielle's bone marrow to heal. She is on the way up!"

Sadly, however, the very next day the count showed that there was a drop in the platelets and Danielle again needed to be transfused. But that little setback couldn't discourage me. I knew full well that she would continue to need transfusions, but my fervent hope was that the need for them would lessen and that they would occur further and further apart. I was confident that she would soon be well enough so we would have other checkers games.

Chapter 17

Depression Sets In

Danielle had lost interest in the things that used to make her happy and she seemed very sad. Even her two favorite nurses noticed a big change in her. Cindy, the day nurse, had taken care of her from the very first day that she checked into Hurley Hospital. Danielle adored Cindy, who treated her like her own daughter.

I was especially thankful for the one night nurse that she had become very close to. If Danielle had a big test coming up or had gone through a very bad day in the hospital, I spent the night with her. Otherwise I went home to be with Cole, Casey and Mark. It was hard for me to leave but the babies needed my attention and I needed a break from the stress at the hospital. My conscience bothered me when I wasn't there and, as a result, I thought, "I get to leave but she doesn't. This is her life twenty-four hours a day and seven days a week. I shouldn't have a break from it either." The night nurse would often sit with Danielle for a while when I was gone and would even sneak ice cream in when she felt like eating.

Eventually Danielle no longer wanted to play games with me and wouldn't leave her room. All she cared about doing was lying in bed. I talked to the doctor about the situation and he explained that she was becoming depressed from being an in-patient for so long. I asked him what we could do about it. "Could I take Danielle outside the hospital for a while to the grassy area in the back?" I asked. Instead, he wanted to give her an anti-depressant, but I was against putting her on still more drugs.

After a time the doctor offered to allow Danielle four-hour passes out of the hospital. I thought that it would be like taking field trips. That sounded good to me; so the very next morning I drove to Flint, picked her up and brought her home for a couple of hours. I know it did her a lot of good to get out of there for a while. But, surprisingly, it was hard on me. It made me remember all over again what it was like having Danielle home and it made me miss her even more.

On the drive back to the hospital, Danielle said to me, "Mom, I miss _me_!" I realized that she was missing her own life. She had been stripped of almost everything and felt that she was not even herself anymore. Danielle's entire life consisted of running to and from clinics for months on end and, lately, of lying in a hospital bed for an entire month. No wonder she was missing herself!

The next morning the doctors took another x-ray of Danielle's lung to see if the ampiterisan B had helped clear up the spot of pneumonia. The results showed no change which was both good and bad. Bad because it had not cured it; good because at least it hadn't gotten any worse. The doctors also decided to discontinue injecting the ampiterisan B by IV and, instead, planned to give her the same drug in pill form, which she could take orally. While Danielle was connected to the IV, she had to stay in the hospital, but if the pill did what it was supposed to, then she could come home.

When I arrived at the hospital the following morning, I found out that one of the counts from Danielle's complete blood count had gone up on its own from fifty to one hundred fifty-six overnight! I thought, "Oh my goodness! Thank you, God, for that sign. She is going to be okay. We just have to get through all the bumps on the way there!"

About that same time, the doctors began giving Danielle potassium supplements to swallow in pill form. Her potassium level had dropped until it was far too low. The pills were extremely large and difficult to swallow, so she asked if she could eat bananas instead. The doctor laughed and said, "You couldn't eat enough bananas in an entire day to get the same amount of potassium that is in one pill." Her depression seemed as if it had lifted a little, because she accepted that with few complaints.

Chapter 18

The Biopsy

I noticed that when Danielle was taken off the ampiterisan B, the doctors had not started her on the oral replacement as they planned. When she had been without the antibiotic for three days, I became worried; especially because her cough seemed to be getting worse again. At that point they suggested doing a biopsy on the spot of pneumonia in her lung.

Because I was upset and frustrated with the way Danielle's treatment was being handled at Hurley, I called Johns Hopkins Hospital again and was able to talk to Dr. Brodsky like I had before. I explained to him what was going on at present and his response was just what I expected. He said, "No, Danielle should not have been taken off the ampiterisan B." He felt that she should be given the antibiotic for another two to four weeks. Also, he said that it might take more time than that before we would see improvements in her blood counts.

The doctor reminded me that his report on the clinical trials had stated it could be as long as ninety-five days after the patient receives chemotherapy before an improvement in the complete blood count would be seen. Danielle had not reached that point as yet. I told Dr.

Inoue and Dr. O what the Baltimore doctor had said. They ignored me on that subject but really pressed me to allow the biopsy. They wanted to know what kind of infection was in her lung so they would know how to treat it. Because I felt I needed more time to think about it and to talk it over with Danielle, I asked them to wait.

Apparently the doctors disagreed with the idea of giving Danielle and me time to decide on the procedure because they asked the pediatric surgeon to explain it to me. The surgeon really scared me. He indicated that he would be on standby call during the biopsy because fifty percent of the patients experience a lung collapse which requires a chest tube to re-inflate it. I was frightened and didn't know what to do about the decision. After talking about it with Danielle, we decided to go ahead with it. I reasoned this way, "The biopsy will give the doctors the information they need and will help them treat the infection."

During my talks with the doctors I had learned some things about the test. Danielle would be heavily sedated. After that the attendants would slide her into a CAT scanner. The machine would display computerized pictures for the doctors to help guide them in the procedure. Then they would use a long needle to probe through her back to the infected spot on her lung and take a sample. The dangerous time would be while the sample was being taken, because the needle might puncture the lung causing it to collapse.

Danielle was scheduled to have the biopsy on September 13th. The night before the procedure, I stayed with her and we both tried to sleep in her narrow hospital bed. It was nearly impossible, but it was funny, too. Before going to sleep we talked for a while and I told Danielle that I wished that I could go through all of the tests in her place. It always amazed me to see how strong she was.

Danielle, for a change, mentioned that she was feeling hungry but they weren't allowing her to eat until after the biopsy. I asked her, "What sounds good that you would really like to eat?"

"KFC honey barbeque strips," she answered.

"Okay," I said, "That is what you are going to have tomorrow right after you are finished with the test."

In the morning we both waited nervously for someone to take Danielle down to the procedure room. Finally, a nurse came and transported her in her hospital bed. We went down in the elevator, around several corners and then followed a long hallway. At the end of the hallway was a door with "CAT" on it. She was wheeled into the room and the door closed.

I was not allowed in the procedure room while the biopsy was going on. Instead, I sat in the chair that was nearest to the door in order to hear any little noise from within. No one else was waiting there so I leaned nearer the door. When I finally realized what I was doing, I said to myself, "This is crazy. You're driving yourself crazy! Why don't you leave and go get the KFC meal you promised to Danielle when she gets out of the test?" I even answered myself by thinking, "Good idea. I can't just sit here like this. I may as well go and get her something that she really wants." I realized that it wasn't much but at least I was doing something for her.

While I was looking for a KFC restaurant, I drove all over Flint. At last I located one but it was in really bad area of the city. There were bars on the windows and thick bullet-proof glass between the customers and the cashier. It was scary but I had to have the meal, so I walked in and nervously stood in line. I was very frightened but tried not to look like it as I ordered the food.

After returning to the hospital, I found Danielle back in her own room and just coming out from under the sedation. As I talked to her,

I asked how it went and if she hurt anywhere. She couldn't remember any of it. Thank goodness, she was one of the fifty percent of patients who had no problem and, therefore, did not need a chest tube. To me that was a huge blessing!

I stayed with Danielle the rest of the day. That evening she had to go for one more x-ray in order to make certain her lung remained inflated. When they wheeled her out of her room for that, I kissed her and told her I loved her and then went home for the night. Each time I leave her, I call from home just before bedtime. When I called that night, she told me that the x-ray result was good and also that we would be given the biopsy report the next day. I was able to go to bed feeling at peace.

Chapter 19

The Wake Up Call

The news was not good when I arrived at Hurley the next morning. The biopsy showed that Danielle had a type of pneumonia called aspergillus. That is a fungus which is constantly in the air and we all breathe it regularly. However, when a person's immune system has been compromised with chemotherapy for a long period of time, the fungus can settle in the body and create trouble. That is what had happened in Danielle's case and it caused the spot of pneumonia on her lung. The doctors began treating her with an antibiotic again and informed me that she would have to remain in the hospital for at least another two to three weeks.

Then the doctors asked to speak to me privately in the hallway. There they explained that Danielle quite possibly may need surgery to remove the spot on the lung. I became very nervous when they went on to state that in case they do the surgery, they don't remove only the spot, but the entire lobe of the lung where it is found. They added that because of her lack of a functioning immune system in addition to her lack of platelets for clotting her blood, operating was not a good option. It would be put off for at least a while, unless the spot became life threatening.

I told them that I realized that the lung was a major organ and asked if she would be all right in case they removed an entire lobe. The setback really bothered me and I wondered why it happened when she had been doing so well. The doctors told me a little more about it. They said that in case the pneumonia traveled through her tissues it might reach a major blood vessel. That would cause internal bleeding and she could bleed to death. They warned me that the sign to watch for was her coughing up blood. All the information that they related frightened me badly. I protested to them about much of it, but I think that it was only because I was so scared.

At that point it was up to me to go back into Danielle's room and explain in a quiet and calm way everything that could happen to her. I really wanted to scream instead. When I did tell her, she asked some questions which I answered the best I could from what the doctors had told me. She seemed to be taking it all right. Actually Danielle's spirits were quite good considering all the bad news she was receiving. I think that those mini four-hour passes out of the hospital had done a world of good for her.

Still another added concern for me was that the doctors asked to do another bone marrow biopsy on Danielle. I refused. She had been through so much lately that I just wanted to give her a break. She hated the biopsies because they were very painful. I wanted the doctors to give her a few more days of peace before they put her through any more tests. As far as I was concerned, that biopsy was not urgent nor was it an immediate concern.

Again the doctors sent in their reinforcement. The pediatric surgeon who had placed Danielle's port and had been on standby during her lung biopsy showed up to ask if he could speak with me. I wondered if it had been suggested by the other doctors because I was being uncooperative with them about the bone marrow biopsy. He asked me to step out of the room and led me to an empty procedure room where we could talk privately.

He began by telling me how serious the situation was. I was thunderstruck when he indicated that he gave Danielle only a fifty percent chance of surviving <u>with</u> or <u>without</u> the surgery on her lung! He explained, "In her present circumstance, she might not live through the surgery, but without the surgery it might be only a short time before the pneumonia spread." I began to cry and simply couldn't stop. Through my sobs I said to him, "I have always asked for Danielle's help in deciding on her treatment. I've been honest with her about all that was going on with her except for <u>one</u> thing. And, that one thing was that she could <u>die</u> from the disease. I never wanted her to have it in her head or her heart that <u>that</u> could even be a possibility."

During the rest of our conference I calmed down a little, but at that moment I actually hated him. I hated him and didn't want to look at him any longer. He left the room and I sat down to be by myself for a while. I cried for a long time as I went over everything in my mind. I thought about how this whole situation came to be, how far we had come and all that we had been through. I'm not sure how long I stayed in that procedure room but I remember that once a nurse walked in to get something and said, "Oh, I'm so sorry. I didn't know anyone was in here." "It's all right." I replied. She asked if she could do anything for me but I answered "No."

I realized that I didn't really hate the doctor as a person, but just hated him for telling me that Danielle had only a fifty percent chance of survival. I hated him for giving me a wake up call to reality.

Chapter 20

Wigged Out

The following day, Doctor Inoue and Doctor O called a meeting and, of course, invited me. After all of us were seated around a table in the conference room, I suddenly realized what was happening. The only reason for the get-together was that I had refused to allow Danielle to have another bone marrow biopsy. They were ganging up on me in order to make me change my mind! I was furious! The meeting turned out to be rather short because it came to an abrupt end when my answer was still, "No, not yet!"

After going through all of that, I felt depressed and angry. Fortunately, Danielle had been given a four-hour pass out of the hospital that day, so I decided that we both needed to have a little fun. As we were leaving, Cindy, Danielle's favorite day nurse, came down the hallway. Cindy took care of Danielle like a second mom when I was not there. Her kind concern always relieved my mind and made me feel so good. When she saw us, Cindy kissed the top of Danielle's bald head and said, "See you when you get back."

That gave me an idea. We would go shopping for Danielle's wig! Over the next few hours we went to four different shops. She tried on wig after wig and looked at hundreds of others. We had a ball! At the last shop we visited, Danielle found one that she just loved. I couldn't understand what she saw in that particular wig because it had no bangs in front, its hair was all one length, and it looked far too large on her tiny head. When Danielle put it on, a huge smile appeared on her face and she just couldn't stop running her fingers through it. How could I say "No" to her?

Danielle was so excited about the new wig that she insisted on wearing it on the way back to the hospital. When we got there, Cindy came into her room to admire it. She acted as if it was the best wig in the world for her. She told Danielle how beautiful she looked wearing it. I was in the hallway near the door when Cindy came out. We just had to smile at one another because of the wig. We were thinking the same thoughts about the thing. Nonetheless, it made Danielle happy and that was very important. After that I only remember seeing her wear the wig a couple of times. I think that it bothered her scalp.

I don't know if it was because of the wig shopping or not, but on October 3rd I finally gave the okay for Danielle to have another bone marrow biopsy. I knew that eventually it would have to happen so that the doctors could find out how the marrow was progressing.

I guess you could say that the test result gave us a bit of good news. It showed that the marrow was at the same level it had been when Danielle was first tested on May 16th, nearly five months previously. Apparently the chemotherapy had completely wiped out the old marrow and new marrow had grown back to the former level. Our hope was that it would continue to grow. The doctor also said that some of the cells in the new marrow were healthier than in the old, so there actually was an ever-so-slight recovery. Any good news was very welcome at the time.

Chapter 21

A Howling Good Time

Over the next few days I watched as Danielle's ANC (Absolute Neutrophil Count) rose from 395 to 590 and then to 900. The Neutrophils are the parts of the white blood cells that help fight off infections. It seemed as if she was finally making some baby steps toward being cured. Then on October 11th her ANC suddenly dropped back down to 392. What a setback! It seemed as if she would go two steps forward then one back. The only things that kept our spirits up were the short four-hour passes out of the hospital that she was still being allowed. We always tried to find something interesting to do during those passes even if it was only a short visit home for Danielle.

One day my grandmother came to the hospital to visit Danielle and me. She told us that she would like to organize a benefit dinner to help pay for some of our expenses. I felt very uncomfortable about asking people for money but we certainly would be able to use it. Commuting daily back and forth between Vassar and Flint was expensive and that was on top of all the other costs we were experiencing. Grandma suggested that the dinner might be held during the first week in November. That was still a couple of weeks away so I thought, "We might not even need it by then." That was wishful thinking but there were some few indications that it might come true.

On October 12th the doctors did another CAT scan of Danielle's lung and that time the results showed the pneumonia lesion had decreased in size. The original scan had shown that it was 2 centimeters across and the second showed that it had diminished to only a little over half that size at 1.2 centimeters. Also her ANC rose to 630. Once again I became very excited and thought, "My girl is getting better! She has gone through a lot—everything from chemotherapy, biopsies and painful tests to infusions of Ampiterisan B—but now all that seems almost worthwhile because recovery seems within sight!" For the following week Danielle's white blood count (WBC) averaged 2 and her ANC count stayed above 1000.

During the middle of October it began to look and feel very festive around Danielle's hospital room. By that time the small space had been her home for a full two months and it had been transformed into her own little apartment. She had things in her room that many patients didn't usually have—such as her own microwave oven and even a mini refrigerator. Besides that I had brought a number of her own things from our house in order to help make her feel more at home. It was a blessing to be able to have all this to make her feel more comfortable.

I think that Danielle began to feel a little blue because Halloween was so close. There were constant reminders everywhere with decorations going up all over the hospital. We hung some of them in her room as well. Because Danielle was getting older, that Halloween probably would be the last year for her to go trick or treating. Certain things about growing up can be a little sad for children. I tried to think of something that might cheer her up.

At a business place, Huckleberry Railroad and Crossroads Village, near the hospital, they were allowing children to trick or treat each night through Halloween. Thinking that Danielle might enjoy that, I asked the doctors if it would be all right for her to participate. They said, "Sure." I drove home to dress Cole and Casey in their costumes. We also picked up another for Danielle and the three of us went back to the hospital to get her dressed in it. Her costume was a big orange pumpkin. We all had a great time stuffing it with hospital pillows to make it look like a nice full, fat pumpkin. We put makeup on her face and she wore a hat that looked as though it had vines sprouting from its top. All three of the children looked so cute in their outfits. The nurses even stopped into Danielle's room to admire all of them before we started out on our night of trick or treating.

On the actual day of Halloween, the doctors gave Danielle a four-hour pass so that I could bring her home to go trick or treating with Cole and Casey in Vassar. As we were leaving the hospital, we talked about the other kids who were patients too, but who were unable to leave the premises. We wondered what we could do for them. I thought of an idea. What if Danielle brought Halloween to them by trick or treating in reverse? She loved the idea. That night we filled treat bags with all kinds of candy and took them with us to the hospital. I stood in the hallway holding the bags and Danielle knocked on the doors and said, "Trick or treat!" Then she walked in and handed each child a bag of candy. It was a lot of fun and turned out to be a howling good time for everyone.

Danielle and Cole

Danielle, Cole and Casey

Danielle in her pumpkin costume

Mark and I

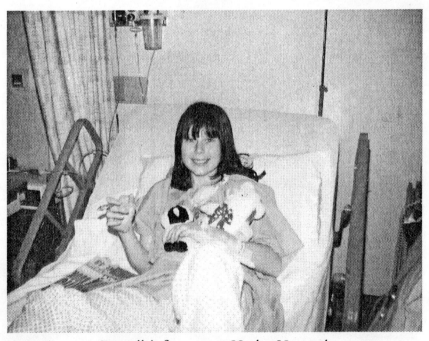

Danielle's first stay at Hurley Hospital

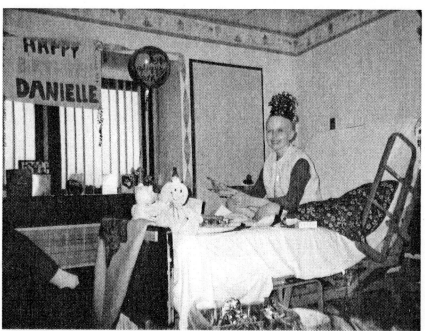

Danielle's birthday party at Hurley

My Grandma, Bill Williams (my father-in-law), Carole Inman, and Danielle at her party

Dan Ward and Danielle in their "bald is..." t-shirts

Danielle in her "bald is beautiful" t-shirt

My sister, Alisha, at her wedding with Danielle

My grandma and Danielle at the fundraising dinner

My mom and Danielle at the dinner

Danielle at school with a few of her friends

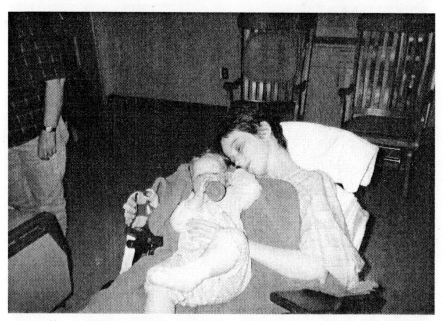

Danielle and Casey cuddled together. This is a couple of months after she was flight cared to Ann Arbor Hospital.

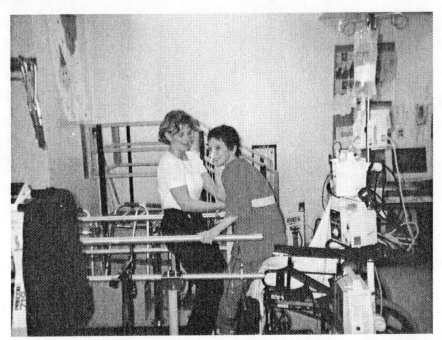

Danielle learning to walk again with her therapist

Danielle playing dress up

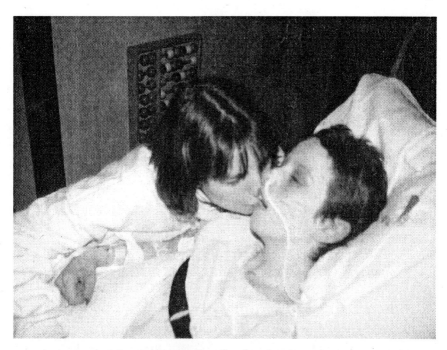

Me and Danielle after her lung surgery

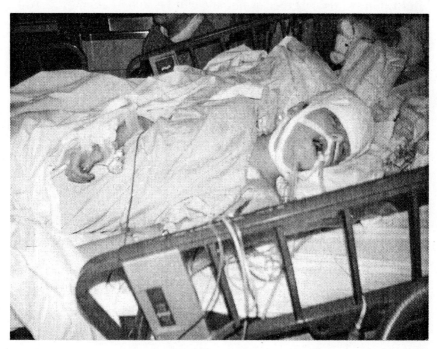

One of Danielle's ICU visits in Ann Arbor

Chapter 22

A Dinner For Danielle

The next time I talked to my grandmother, she told me that Danielle's benefit dinner was planned for November 5th. Because I had some doubts, I said, "But, Grandma, Danielle is still in the hospital and I don't know whether or not she will be able to attend it." After I approached the doctors to ask permission, they said that they would make every attempt to see that she was able to be there. We were all very much encouraged because Danielle's ANC (Absolute Neutrophil Count) was staying about 2000 and her WBC (White Blood Count) was between 3 and 4. Both of those were very positive signs.

The day of the dinner arrived and Danielle was given a short pass out of the hospital to attend it. The dinner was planned for 5 p.m. at the FOE (Fraternal Order of Eagles) hall in Vassar. That afternoon I drove to Hurley and picked her up. Because there would be a crowd of people at the dinner, Danielle had to wear a face mask to protect her from germs in the air. The turnout at the benefit dinner was unbelievable, at least partly because Johnny Burke made an announcement about it on his radio program WHNN.

Johnny Burke was a local DJ who organized a fund for sick children. When he would hear of youngsters in our area who needed financial assistance because of illness, he would contact them and try to help. Back in September, Johnny had called Danielle and me at the hospital one morning and we both were able to talk live on the radio with him. That was very exciting and on that day she became one of "Johnny's Kids." Then he donated a thousand dollars to us in order to help pay some of our expenses.

Another reason for the large turnout at the benefit dinner was that my grandmother was a member of the Fraternal Order of Eagles and not only did the local members come, but others from neighboring towns did also. Many of the people there didn't even know us but still put money in the donation jars. I was deeply touched as I watched all those generous people showing in some way that they cared about my beautiful daughter.

Before the benefit was quite finished, I had to interrupt it to take Danielle back to the hospital. She had only been given a four-hour pass and, even then, the doctors still had to postpone some of her medications until she returned. She seemed to get through all the festivities and excitement of the dinner very well. For that I was thankful.

On November 9th, four days after the dinner, Danielle was able to check out of the hospital. At first, it seemed really strange to have her home again but that didn't last very long. As soon as she was at home, she wanted to go back to school once more because she really missed her friends. I checked with the school officials and they said that they would be happy to have her return. The school people fully cooperated in every way to help Danielle and they always were very good to us. They even organized and held two different fund raisers for us. Vassar is a small town and so I was really amazed at the number of generous and giving people who lived there.

Chapter 23

Meeting The DJ

Though it continued to be necessary for us to make the daily drive to the hospital clinic in Flint for blood count checks and transfusions, it seemed wonderful that Danielle didn't have to stay overnight. She still received the daily neupogen shots in her legs. That was the medication for helping her ANC (Absolute Neutrophil Count) and WBC (White Blood Count) to come up. The results from the most recent Complete Blood Count (CBC) showed her ANC was 5,214 and her WBC was 6.6—both were very high compared to what they had been. Because of the improvement, the doctors decided that the neupogen shots could be decreased so that they were only given on Mondays, Wednesdays and Fridays. Even if it was just slight, each little change did show progress was being made. For that I was thankful. The only dark cloud on the horizon was that Danielle's Red Blood Count (RBC) hadn't shown very much improvement.

One day while we were driving to the hospital clinic, we heard on the radio that the DJ, Johnny Burke, was holding a fundraiser at a mall near the hospital. That seemed like a good opportunity for us, so I said to Danielle, "Boo, maybe if you don't have to have a transfusion today, we could go to the mall and meet Johnny." Danielle had wanted to meet him personally ever since they had talked on the radio together. She immediately became very excited about that possibility.

Unfortunately the blood count results that day showed that Danielle did need an infusion of platelets. So it was very late when we finally left the hospital for the mall and we were not sure if Johnny would still be there. But, we went anyway. When we got there we found out that the fundraiser was right in the middle of the mall and learned that he, in fact, was still there! I had Cole and Casey in a stroller and Danielle at my side as we walked up to the big gathering.

They had set up a huge tent for the event in an open space and, when we approached it, I couldn't see Johnny anywhere. We met his co-host, Jodi, who said, "Just wait a minute. He'll be right back." He appeared a little later and Jodi said to him, "There is someone here who would like to meet you." He looked at us and said, "Yes?" I introduced the two of them by saying, "Johnny, this is one of your kids. Meet Danielle Tausch." His reply was, "Oh, Danielle. Come inside the tent." Then he gave her a big hug.

Danielle sat on a couch in the tent with Johnny and Jodi while all of them visited. They had ordered dinner to be delivered and invited us to stay and eat with them. But, before the food arrived, one of the babies made a big mess in its diaper and we had to leave in a hurry. Johnny made a wisecrack about the terrible odor. That relieved our embarrassment a little and we all laughed about the incident.

Once outside the mall, while walking back to our van, I asked Danielle, "Well, what did you think?" She answered, "Jodi is really pretty, but Johnny is older than I thought he would be." We laughed even more. All of us had a great time finally meeting with Johnny Burke, the DJ.

Chapter 24

The Roller Coaster Ride

Driving each day to the hospital and enduring the constant ups and downs of the laboratory reports were starting to get to me. My feelings at that time are very difficult to describe. I began to sense that I was more and more isolated, almost as if I were trapped in one little corner of my own mind. No one was able to really understand me or my feelings. People seemed unable to reach out to me. There were people all around me constantly but they didn't hear my inner screaming and they couldn't sense the pounding of my heart. "If only they knew how to reach me." I thought. My mom told me that I pushed people away, but I don't know how I did that. Silently I begged, "Please, someone, just understand me!"

One day Danielle and I were returning to Hurley after a four-hour pass out of the hospital. While we waited at the elevator to go up to the second floor, she began to feel sick to her stomach from the medication she had been given. Even though there were a number of people waiting there, Danielle just couldn't hold it and started throwing up in the canister between the elevator doors. I felt terrible for her and ran to the bathroom to get a cool, damp cloth.

When we were on the elevator, Danielle continued to feel sick and without any energy so she sat on the floor for the trip up. Another passenger, a lady who had gotten on when we did, said, "He doesn't look like he feels very good." (Danielle was still bald from the chemotherapy.) I immediately bristled and snapped, "He is a she!" Though it wasn't her fault, the lady apologized.

At rare times there were some lighthearted things that happened because of Danielle's baldness. At about the same time as she had undergone chemotherapy, the husband of my best friend was also treated with it. Both Danielle and Dan became bald at the same time. I purchased two t-shirts, one for each of them. One of them said "Bald is Beautiful!" and the other said "Bald is Sexy!" When I gave the t-shirts to them they put them on and looked really cute together. I took a picture of the two of them in their shirts.

Somewhere in the back of my mind I realized that Christmas was coming soon. I didn't think much about it and, to be brutally honest, had no idea how much of the Christmas shopping had been done. The one and only thing I really wanted for Christmas was good news about Danielle's recovery and a happy healthy family. Though I didn't feel much of the seasonal spirit, I did want to try to make that particular Christmas special for Danielle. After all, she had a hard year and deserved some happiness. Danielle had asked for a television set with a VCR built into it for her bedroom, so Mark and I bought that as her one big gift. I must confess that I was at least a little eager to watch her reaction when she opened her present.

Besides the two Hurley Hospital doctors, Danielle also was still under the care of Dr. Abella in Detroit. Consequently we had to make occasional trips there for checkups with him. We had been told ahead of time that during the December 7th appointment the doctor planned to have her undergo another bone marrow biopsy for his records. I asked my father-in-law, Bill, to go along to sit with Danielle during the procedure. I just couldn't stand to hold her hand that time. It was too gut-wrenching for me as a mom to hear my child in agonizing pain and not be able to soothe her in any way.

We all went into the procedure room before the nurse practitioner arrived. When she got there, I waited for the last minute before it was to begin and then went to the waiting room. I was supposed to stay there until they were done with the biopsy. After the procedure was started, I couldn't tolerate sitting there, so I walked down the hallway toward the room where they were. At that moment I heard Danielle scream and start to cry. I threw the door open and yelled, "Can't you give her something more for the pain?" The nurse ignored me as she worked quickly. "I'm almost done," she said. And she was. That was the quickest biopsy that Danielle had been through, but it also was the hardest on her.

Later the nurse explained the reason for that. She said, "The more biopsies children have, the more sensitive their nerves can become, so they are more painful." Afterward Danielle was required to lie on her stomach for about fifteen minutes to make certain that the bleeding from the incision stopped. Because she hadn't been able to have anything to eat or drink until the biopsy was over, I helped her eat a snack and drink a little as she lay there.

For the next part of her checkup, Danielle was to go down the hallway to another section of the hospital for an x-ray. The nurse put a big gauze patch over her biopsy incision and we walked to the x-ray department. At the reception window, I signed her in and we sat down to wait our turn. A few moments later Danielle said, "Mom, the back of my pants feels really wet." I told her to stand and, sure enough, the blood had not clotted and her entire back and bottom were soaked with it.

"We'll be back. I have to take Danielle to the clinic again," I explained to the lady at the x-ray window. At the clinic we got help right away. The nurse on duty took her into a room and had her lie on her stomach again. Then the nurse placed pressure on the wound non-stop for fifteen minutes. That seemed to work because at the end of that time there was no more oozing blood. Once again we returned to the x-ray department and that time made it through fine.

When we met with Dr. Abella, we received the best Christmas present we could have asked for. He told us that Danielle's bone marrow was showing recovery. "Yes!," I thought. My excitement was very hard to contain. The doctor took us across the hallway where the microscopes were kept. He showed us the slides from her first biopsy and then compared them to those from this one. He explained what to look for in the cells on each slide. It was fascinating to examine the cells under the microscope.

There was more good news. Danielle's Absolute Neutrophil Count (ANC) and her White Blood Count (WBC) both were holding steady as a result of the shots she was receiving. The only disappointment was that the Red Blood Count (RBC) continued to drop. Dr. Abella decided to start her on epogen shots which were designed to boost the production of red blood cells. With the addition of that medication, Danielle was then receiving six shots each week in her legs, plus a needle in her shoulder each time they had to access her port. I felt as though I was becoming her nurse because I gave her all the injections and medications. Although, I had never actually done it, I knew every detail of how to access the port and what had to be done when it was accessed. Being able to do those things for Danielle made me feel good. I really needed that.

Two weeks later, on December 21st, we went for the regular clinical visit at Hurley Hospital. There at the laboratory, Danielle's finger was poked with a needle and a sample was drawn. Then, in one of the rooms of the clinic, we were given the results of the Complete Blood Count (CBC) from the sample that had been taken. FOR THE VERY FIRST TIME HER BLOOD COUNTS HELD STABLE ENOUGH THAT SHE REQUIRED NO TRANSFUSION OF ANY KIND! I couldn't believe it! She was able to walk out of the clinic with no transfusion. I was in heaven!

The nurse told us not to come back for a couple of days. That statement made me both nervous and excited at the same time. I was nervous wondering, "Can she really go a couple of days without coming here?" I was also excited thinking, "Yes, she is going to stay away for that long!" Two days after that, on December 23rd, Danielle still did not need a transfusion. However, her blood counts had dropped somewhat. The doctor wanted her to come back the next day, on Christmas Eve for a transfusion then. He felt that it would last for a couple of days, through the holiday.

I am so happy that my precious little girl is recovering. I knew it would happen all along. She had been knocked down a few times, but she always came right back again. We both were on an emotional roller coaster.

Chapter 25

The Battle Becomes Life-threatening

Three days before Christmas, Danielle wanted to spend the night with my mom who had promised to take her Christmas shopping. I gave her permission with the warning that the two of them should be very careful not to tire her out too much. Because she was doing so well, I had started to relax her restrictions a little. After all, she needed to get at least some of her own life back again.

About ten thirty that night the phone rang. "Who is calling this late?" I wondered. When I answered the phone, all I heard was coughing. Finally Danielle was able to choke out, "Mom, I'm coughing up blood!" "Oh, dear God, please NO! Not now!" was all I could think. Quickly I collected myself and said, "Okay, I'm on my way!" I grabbed my coat, purse and keys, told Mark where I was going and ran out the door.

The drive to my mother's house was less than two miles so I was there in just moments. I walked in and found Danielle hanging over the kitchen sink spitting out blood. Mom was still asleep and didn't even know anything about it yet. Danielle had gotten out of bed and called me right away. My first reaction was to call Hurley Hospital and talk to her doctor there. After I had explained what happened, I asked him, "Can I drive her to Flint or should I call an ambulance?" He said that I would have to make that decision because he couldn't see her and couldn't tell how bad she was. I decided to call the ambulance.

By that time the noise had wakened my mother. She came out of her bedroom, saw what was happening to Danielle and gave her a bowl to spit in so that she could sit down. In the very short time that it took me to call the 911 number, she had already filled the bowl a quarter of the way to the top. After I hung up, I tried consoling Danielle by telling her that just to be on the safe side I wanted the ambulance to drive us to Hurley. Actually, I was lying to her, because I remembered back to the surgeon telling me about her fifty percent chance of surviving. I just couldn't tell Danielle that.

She continued to cough and each time had to spit out more blood. Her entire mouth was covered because it ran out of her nose and down her chin. I felt total panic.

Twenty minutes went by and still we heard no siren. What was going on? The ambulance garage was right there in town, for heaven's sake. I began to get upset and called 911 again. The dispatcher told me that the ambulance crew had been paged and they were on their way. The first to arrive was a policeman but all he did was talk with Danielle.

At last, after another ten minutes had passed, the ambulance finally got there. Immediately the emergency medical technicians started Danielle on an IV in order to fill her veins with fluid. By that time she had coughed up more than half a bowlful of blood. They loaded her into the ambulance and got ready to take off. During the trip to the hospital an emergency medical technician, a paramedic and I rode in the back with Danielle.

The paramedic called ahead to the hospital to tell the doctor when we would get there and to fill him in on necessary information about Danielle. I asked him to let the doctor know that she would need an infusion of platelets when we got there in order to stop the bleeding. To myself I prayed, "Please God, let there be some available for her." The roads were snow-covered so the long drive seemed to go on forever.

When we first boarded the ambulance, the medical technician gave Danielle one of the square plastic pans that they carry with them. She began vomiting from the blood going into her stomach and the pan was soon half full. I had never seen so much blood and wondered how one body could hold that much. I fervently hoped that she had enough to hold her until we got to the hospital. The technician asked Danielle her name. When she told her, the lady said, "Well, it's nice to meet you, Danielle. I've heard a lot about you." Apparently because Vassar is a very small town word got around quickly. Our conversation with the technician helped to relax me a little.

We finally arrived at Hurley Hospital and the paramedics took Danielle directly into an emergency room where an ER team was waiting for us. The team doctor took one look at her and said, "Move her to the Trauma Unit." As we hurriedly made our way down the hallway, the doctor explained that he would be inserting tubes to remove the blood from her lungs. I agreed to that. Danielle was having difficulty breathing and gasped, "Please hurry!" She apparently overheard our conversation about what was going on and just wanted the doctor to fix it at once. They wheeled her into a large room with swinging doors made of steel. I couldn't go beyond the doors so I had to wait in the hallway.

Because we had spent so much time at Hurley over the past few months, all the doctors and nurses from the pediatric floor knew us well. They had heard that I was bringing Danielle in that night and that her situation was extremely serious. As I waited outside the Trauma Unit door, I was seldom alone because every so often a nurse from the second floor unit would stop by to check on me and ask if I was okay.

Even a young doctor, who was interning in the hospital and knew Danielle, came down just after we arrived to talk with me for a moment. She said that she was going into the trauma room to be with Danielle and to help her any way she could. I was comforted by that because I knew that Danielle liked her and had spent time with her before. The doctor's face would be a familiar one in the room.

After a time, while I was standing in the hallway waiting for any kind of news, that same doctor came out of the Trauma Unit. I thought, "Oh, good. She'll let me know what is going on in there." I was terribly wrong, though, because she walked right by me as if she didn't know me. As the doctor passed she didn't even look at me but just kept on walking down the hallway. That frightened me more.

By that time some of my family had gotten to the hospital to sit with me during the ordeal. One of the trauma nurses showed us to a private waiting room in the unit. She told us that there was a phone available in case we wished to make calls and also that they would let us know when Danielle was stable. Her statement confused me more. I wondered how she could be unstable when all she needed were the platelets and the chest tubes to drain off the blood. While I was mulling that over in my mind, another pediatric nurse from upstairs came in to hug me and asked if she could do anything for me. I told her "No," that I was okay, but just wanted to know what was going on in there.

At last one of the Trauma Unit doctors approached us and made an announcement. He said that they had decided to Flight Care Danielle in the helicopter to the Ann Arbor hospital. My thoughts were a jumble. "Hold on. Flight Care? That must mean that she is in really bad shape! But she's not that bad. She should be okay now that she has been given the platelets." And finally I thought, "I won't be able to go with her on the helicopter." So many things were going on in my mind that I couldn't keep up with them.

The doctor said that I could see Danielle before they put her in the helicopter and he led me into the trauma room. When I walked through the double doors and got my first look at her, I froze. I certainly didn't expect the scene that was in front of me. A nurse was standing behind Danielle holding a bag over her mouth. The nurse was doing Danielle's breathing for her by squeezing the bag. As we came near she squeezed some more and said to the doctor, "This is all I can force in." I knew she meant that was all the air she could push into Danielle's lungs. Another nurse on the other side of the bed was holding a bag of platelets and attempting to get them into Danielle's body. Everyone in the room was doing his or her job. It was noisy, but they were all helping Danielle.

The nurse at Danielle's head jerked me back to reality when she said, "Mom, come and talk to her." When I looked at Danielle's face it was three times its normal size. I was amazed that a person's appearance could change so much in such a short time. I crooned to her, "I'm here Boo. I'm not leaving. I'm staying right here." Her eyes were only halfway open and she was covered with iodine and blood. When I hesitated, the nurse said, "Keep on talking to her."

I asked the nurse why Danielle looked like that. She didn't answer. A different nurse came over and pointed out to me that there was another trauma case coming into the room. She said to ignore what was happening on the other side and continue talking to Danielle. By that time I had run out of things to say to her so I sang Christmas carols instead. Only she could hear me because I was very close to her ear but I wanted her to know that I was there. At that point, two uniformed men walked in. I assumed that they were the helicopter flight crew and were there to get Danielle. Someone, I don't know who, said, "Say goodbye, Mom. It's time to go."

As I left the emergency room a security guard asked if my car was in the parking ramp. When I said it was, he offered to drive me to it. I thanked him and accepted the ride. Earlier I had asked God to help Danielle and I thought that he hadn't heard me yet. In the police car the guard showed me I was mistaken. He had a Christian radio station playing and asked, "What is your child's name? I hope you don't mind my asking, but when I pray for children, I like to be able to use their own names." I told him that it was Danielle. I felt that the guard was an answer from God saying, "I am here. I did hear you."

Danielle and the helicopter would get to Ann Arbor in only minutes, but it would take me a couple of hours to drive there, so my mom decided to ride with me. It was getting late and she didn't want me to go alone. It turned out to be a long couple of hours because I passed by one of my exits on the freeway and had to turn around and go back. It was nearly 2 a.m. and I wasn't concentrating on driving. Instead, I was wondering what to expect when we got to the hospital. I was terribly frightened. Was Danielle going to be all right? Either I couldn't accept it or just couldn't comprehend exactly how sick she really was.

Chapter 26

The Intensive Care Unit

It was about 3 a.m. when Mom and I got to the University of Michigan Hospital in Ann Arbor. As I stepped through the door someone said, "Mrs. Tausch?" I answered, "Yes," but wondered how she knew my name or which door I would be entering. It was a large place and I could have come through any door. As we walked down the hallway, she began explaining things to me.

She said that Danielle was in the pediatric part of the Intensive Care Unit. Also, she warned me that when I see her for the first time, it might be a little scary and possibly overwhelming for me. According to her Danielle was stable and resting but she was on life support, which meant that a respirator breathed for her. I had heard of life support systems before but had never actually seen one.

The patients' rooms in the Intensive Care Unit were either in the open space in front of the nurse's desk or behind glass walls. All the rooms circled around the nurse's station in a sort of "U" shape. That way the nurses could always look directly at the patients to make sure that everything was all right with them. The area was very quiet except for an occasional "beep" from a machine or a "hiss" from a respirator.

The lady led me to Danielle's room which was one of the glassed-in types. That was necessary because she lacked an operating immune system and could not be exposed to outside germs. I paused at the door and looked in at her. She appeared to be sleeping and had a tube coming out of her mouth. "I'm all right with this. It doesn't seem so bad." I thought.

But, as I walked closer, a whole new picture appeared. Danielle had the respirator tube in her mouth, two IVs were in her left arm, one in her right arm, another was in the right side of her neck and two were in her groin. There were tubes coming out of each side of her chest in addition to the two from her nose. "How can one little body take all this?" I wondered. It was very scary to see someone I loved so much in that condition. I didn't know what to say or even if I could touch her. My mom had to leave the room for a few moments because she had broken down and was sobbing uncontrollably.

I sat beside Danielle for a while and talked to her. At the time I wondered if it was true that unconscious patient's sense when their loved ones are nearby. If it was true, then I wanted her to know that I was there. I contented myself with holding her hand and rubbing her stomach since they seemed to be only two places on her body that were free from tubes. The terrible night was taking its toll on me. I knew that I wasn't thinking straight because of stress and being so tired. I wasn't merely tired; I was totally exhausted.

On either side of the doors leading into the Intensive Care Unit were rooms for patients' families. The one on the right had a television with several recliners facing it. At the back of that room were small cubicles where family members could lie down and get some rest. The room on the left side of the entrance contained a couch, a table and chairs plus a counter with a coffee pot, a sink and a small refrigerator. Like the room across the way, that one also had a television and several recliners.

Mom and I decided to make ourselves comfortable on the couch or in the recliners because all the sleeping cubicles in the other room were taken. There were family members all over the unit trying to stay close to their sick children. I chose the couch and stretched halfway across it using my purse for a pillow and my coat for a blanket. I simply needed to sleep for a few minutes so that I would have the strength to keep going for Danielle. Though my body desperately needed rest, I stayed wide awake. If I shut my eyes, flashback pictures of Danielle at Hurley Hospital or here in the Intensive Care Unit appeared in my mind's eye. Finally I gave up because there was no point in trying to sleep. I went back to Danielle's room to spend the sleepless hours with her.

Chapter 27

The Christmas Basket

That following afternoon, which was December 23rd, Danielle began waking a little but she still was not coherent at all. The doctors thought possibly she was having seizures so they induced a coma to allow her to rest some more. It became a waiting game during which we would see how well her body could heal itself. The next day, Christmas Eve, they made the decision to let her wake up from the coma.

As she came out of the sedation, Danielle had no memory or understanding of what had happened to her. She soon was awake enough to realize that she wanted the respirator tube taken out of her mouth. That was not possible because the nurse who did the most recent routine suction from her lungs found more fresh blood. Therefore, the doctor hadn't yet made the decision about how long she would have to endure the tube.

Since coming out of the coma, Danielle had experienced uncontrollable jerking and shaking over her entire body. The doctors were not certain of its cause but thought it might be seizures or the reaction to the trauma she had been through recently. I found it very hard to watch what was happening to her.

More tests were ordered for Danielle because the doctors wanted to see if there was damage to the brain or any other part of her body. After they did a whole body CAT scan, the results, at that point, ruled out seizures as the cause of the shaking. That was a big blessing for her.

The doctors kept me informed about everything. They said that their main goal right then was to stabilize Danielle. They also mentioned the possibility of doing lung surgery to remove the spot of pneumonia infection which probably caused the problem. However, considering her present condition, waiting is the only thing that they could safely do right then.

That same day, Christmas Eve, the doctors decided to begin removing the chest tubes one by one. The tubes were supposed to have been placed so that they lay between the lungs and the ribs. But both of them had mistakenly been inserted directly into Danielle's lungs. The doctor explained that the lung might collapse when they pull the tube out, and in case that happened, they would have to re-insert it again, but they would re-insert it where it originally should have been placed.

By 4:30 that afternoon, both chest tubes had been removed without any problem. It was my impression that was another huge blessing for Danielle. I had previously noticed that when there was the possibility of something going wrong during a test or a procedure, Danielle seemed to be singularly blessed because the better of the two choices usually occurred.

Danielle was showing signs of being able to breathe on her own, so the doctors planned to remove the respirator either that evening or the next morning. She was more alert as well but there still were times when she was confused. Not all the news was good because a new complication had arisen. She began running a fever of 105°. The doctors decided that it would not be wise to remove the respirator until the fever broke. We all hoped that after a few more days in the Intensive Care Unit she could be moved to a regular hospital room.

These are some of the things that ran through my mind during the hours I spent in the Intensive Care Unit with Danielle. I really felt that she was going to be fine. Her body just needed time to heal from the trauma it had gone through. After some time passed we would be able to go home and continue our life as it had been only two days ago. We would make the clinic trips again and her bone marrow would go on healing. <u>Danielle would do more than just come out of this Intensive Care Unit! She would beat the aplastic anemia and she would have no side effects!</u> I am overwhelmed by how much I love Danielle; her fight for survival has made me see her through new eyes.

Christmas Eve night was very quiet in the Intensive Care Unit. I sat in a rocking chair near Danielle's bed and occasionally held her hand or caressed her belly. I had turned the television on and a Christmas show was playing. Then my attention was drawn to the doorway where a man and a young boy stood. The boy had a basket in his hand and he brought it over to me. While he did that, the man said, "This is from my son and me. He was here a year ago." I hugged the little boy and then began to cry when I tried to thank him.

After they left, I sat there in the rocking chair with the basket on my lap and thought to myself, "Boo, we are going to do that same thing next year. Children <u>do</u> get out of the Intensive Care Unit and are perfectly healthy afterward." I looked inside the basket and found all sorts of "goodies," There were snacks, magazines, toothpaste, plus other little necessities one might use while waiting for a child to recover. The man and little boy were extremely thoughtful and they touched my heart.

About midnight I decided to go home for a while. I would be back in the morning after I had gotten some sleep. I knew Danielle was in the best place for her and right then she was sleeping really well. Her fight for survival made me see just how very much I loved her. It was almost overwhelming. I kissed her good night, held her hand and told her I loved her and left her in God's hands for the night.

Chapter 28

Did I Miss Christmas?

Christmas morning I awoke early and opened presents with Cole, Casey and Mark. My Christmas with them didn't last long because immediately after that I headed off to the hospital to spend the day with Danielle. When I got there I learned that she had been moved to another room in the Intensive Care Unit. Right after I found her I noticed that there was photograph of Santa and her on the stand next to the bed. Santa had come to visit the children in the unit that morning. I wished I had been there to see that.

Troubling questions had been going through my mind about when Danielle finally did wake up. "Is she going to be my same Danielle? How is she going to act? Will she have a sound mind that is trapped in a handicapped body? Will she be able to communicate with me so I'll know how to help her?" I knew that I was worrying too much about the future when I should have been concentrating on just getting through that day.

Before I got there, the doctors had already removed the respirator and the two IVs from Danielle's groin. The back of her bed was up in a sitting position and she was much more alert than she had been the day before. That alone was a really great Christmas present for me. She tried talking to me but had a very hard time speaking and difficulty remembering things. Nonetheless, because I had been so eager to hear her voice, I thought the raspy little sounds she made were the best sounds I had ever heard. She still had slight fever, but it wasn't as high as it had been.

"Did I miss Christmas?" Danielle asked. I hesitated before answering and she became upset and started to cry. So I told her one more lie. "No, you did not miss Christmas." The fact that she asked that question was a great sign. It meant that she still had her memory and so possibly there had not been any brain damage.

Later that day, in a conversation with one of the ICU nurses, I learned some things I didn't know before. She said, "That night Danielle was brought in, there was talk all around the unit that a new patient was coming but they didn't expect her to live through the night."

I thought to myself, "They didn't know Danielle's spirit like I did. I knew what she had already battled through and I just didn't feel in my heart that I would lose her that night."

The nurse also added, "At Hurley Hospital, Danielle had gone into cardiac arrest for a few moments and that is why they were worried about possible brain damage."

I thought that it was very strange but no one had told me about any of that before the nurse did.

Then the realization came to me about why the interning doctor at Hurley had walked right past me without speaking when I was waiting for news outside the Trauma Room. Danielle apparently had arrested and the doctor simply did not want to be the one to tell me Danielle might not make it. At that point I understood her feelings.

Just seeing Danielle sitting up in bed and trying to talk to me made me feel that everything was all right. Both tubes were still in her nose—

the one for feeding her and the other to drain the blood out of her stomach. She could lift her right arm a little, but could not move either her left arm or left leg. Her body continued with the jerking movements which the doctors still couldn't explain. One of their theories was that she had chorea, which is a series of small strokes. A doctor from the Neurology Department was scheduled to see her the next day.

That same day the doctor removed the draining tube from Danielle's nose and left the feeding tube in place. It had to remain until they knew that she could eat and keep the food down. They ordered a dinner tray of all clear liquids and then asked me to feed her. They wanted to see if she could tolerate that type of food without throwing it up. It was a test to see if the feeding tube could be removed. The dinner consisted of chicken broth, Jell-O, juice and a Popsicle. I was determined to prove to them that Danielle was going to be all right and that they could take the tube out of her nose.

I began feeding Danielle small bites from the tray. I wanted so much for her to be able to keep the food down. If she couldn't, then it would seem like another failure—a further setback. I urged her on, "Come on, Boo, we have to do this to get that tube taken out. We have to prove that you can eat. I know that you can do this!" Then all of a sudden it all came back up! I was heartbroken. I wanted that tube <u>out</u>. I wanted her to be normal again!

The next morning, which was the day after Christmas, I noticed that there were no more tremors. They had stopped on their own overnight. Hurray! Danielle could move her arms and legs a slight bit better but still didn't have complete control over them. She could only lift them up, down or sideways—nothing more.

Danielle's long-term memory about the past was good, but her short-term memory about things she had been told five minutes ago, was not nearly as good. That day she also complained about not being able to see. I tried to comfort her by explaining that she had been through a serious trauma and that it would take time for her body to heal. We experienced a problem with communicating so I tried asking her only yes or no questions. For example, I asked, "Is it a black blindness?" Her answer was, "No." I tried asking more questions but we were not able to talk very well. Why that was happening was a mystery to me.

When Danielle started waking up a doctor from the Neurology Department came to see her once or twice each day. The neurologist ordered an electroencephalogram (EEG) which tests the brain waves but I haven't as yet heard what the results showed.

A day or so later, I noticed a big change in Danielle. She was very groggy and sleepy—not alert like she had been. I missed her terribly when she was like that but still felt that everything was going to turn out fine. Over and over I said to myself, "We just need to give her body a little more time to heal—it has been through a lot."

On the morning of December 27th, we noticed that Danielle had gotten much worse overnight. She was not responding at all. The Intensive Care doctor ordered an MRI and a spinal tap hoping for some answers. Danielle also underwent a CAT scan of her brain and the results from that test showed that there was some swelling.

I was at a loss about what I could do to help Danielle so I moved the tubes and lines out of my way and lay beside her in the bed the way we once did. I rubbed her belly and held her hand just to let her know that I was there. I noticed that her hair, which was beginning to grow back, was then about an inch long and it looked a little curly.

While lying there with Danielle, I thought about the whole situation. When she first woke from the coma, there were a couple of negative things going on with her body. They seemed like small things that would get better when she had time to heal. Instead of that happening, she was getting worse. That's just not fair! I had known early on that there was a chance of brain damage, but I didn't think it could happen a few days after her trauma. Not, when she had already been awake, talking to me and seeming to be almost normal. For once I would simply like things to move forward smoothly.

Chapter 29

The Battle Rages On

The neurologist who had been treating Danielle came to her room and asked to talk to me. At the time I was lying down with her, so I sat up on the side of the bed to have our conversation. After introducing himself, he asked, "What was she like?"

His question upset me terribly and I looked at him and began to cry. I tried not to but couldn't help it. I wasn't able to answer right away but finally choked out, "She was a normal fifth grader who loved to listen to music, to dance, to have her friends visit us, and to go to their homes to visit." Then I continued to sob.

The doctor stood there and listened to me. People usually just don't understand that Danielle was a normal pre-teen girl before coming to the hospital. The neurologist was the exception because he did try to understand. Of all the others he seemed to be one of the few who reached out to me and did comprehend the situation. In a kindly way, he explained the results of the MRI to me. He indicated that the test showed that there was damage to both the basal lobe and the occipital lobe of Danielle's brain. <u>Brain damage</u>. Someone had actually said it and confirmed that it was true. The doctor went on to say that she would probably have to re-learn the motor skills again because there was more damage than originally thought. To me, other than her forgetfulness and not being able to see, she seemed fine.

One day Danielle woke up but she did not really "wake up" in the usual sense. Her body and face both looked as though they were awake but she was not coherent. She began to have tremors across her entire body and her eyes continually jerked up and to the right. To me it appeared as if she were having seizures. The doctors didn't understand what was going on either. They had decided that, for a time, they would just watch her carefully in order to see what would happen next. During our long wait I finally asked a nurse, "Wouldn't it be possible that her body would eventually become so exhausted from the constant movement that it would have to rest and then the tremors would come to an end?" She didn't have an answer for me.

Several members of our family came to see Danielle and to be with me during the long wait. Only two people at a time were allowed to be in the room with ICU patients, so we took turns throughout the night going in to sit with her.

Because I had a lot of time to sit and think, I remembered an earlier incident. A couple of days ago a nurse had to draw blood from Danielle's port when she had a fever. The blood sample would be tested to see if an infection was present. The nurse had not used that type of port previously, so I sat on the bed beside her and tried to help. All of a sudden it dawned on me that the nurse had not used the proper procedures while accessing the port. She just pulled the needle out afterward. She should have flushed it with a saline solution to keep it clean and then with heparin to prevent clotting. Because of that nurse's one careless draw, Danielle's port was probably rendered useless. That was upsetting to me along with the rest of the situation.

By December 28th, Danielle had not slept for two days. The body tremors continued and so did the jerky eye movements. As if all of that were not enough, one of her nurses told me that there was another problem. Danielle's heart rate had dipped down into the sixties. The doctors were still trying to figure out what was happening with her. Right now it seemed as though she was experiencing one complication after another.

Danielle's battle with her disease had taken its toll on me as well. I was consumed with everything about her. Because I felt she needed me, her ICU room became my entire world. I thought of nothing else other than how I could help her. Slowly the realization came to me that I had to take a break from it or I would go crazy. I hoped that Danielle would understand when I decided to go home for a while. I missed Cole and Casey and felt too stressful to stay another night.

I didn't go to see Danielle the next day. Instead I spent it at home with the babies, but my thoughts continually were on her. The following day I told her I was sorry that I had missed a day of visiting her. Everyone probably thought I was a terrible mom but I just couldn't bring myself to go to the hospital that day.

The day I returned there was a big improvement in Danielle's condition. When I asked her questions, she blinked her eyes to answer. She was more stable and the shakes and tremors had disappeared. However, she was extremely emotional and cried often. The neurologist told me that over time she should make even more of an improvement than she was showing then. He and the other doctors were talking of moving her out of the Intensive Care Unit to a regular room that evening. I felt that every day she would move forward toward recovery.

Up until then Danielle was unable to have a roommate in her ICU room, but that had changed. In the other bed there was a boy who was probably a year younger than she was. His head was completely wrapped and there was a tube extending from the bandages on top. Someone told me that he was in a snowmobile accident and had been transported to Ann Arbor by helicopter.

Quietly I stood in the hall and looked through the window at Danielle and the boy. The boy's father sat at the bedside, his head bowed in prayer and he held a Bible in his hands. I <u>knew</u> that the little boy was going to make it. I could just feel it. His father's faith was so strong that it would heal him. That made me question myself. Is my faith strong enough to get Danielle through this? Am I trusting in God enough to see her through? I talked to Him every day and asked for His help and thanked Him for each small blessing. I wondered, "Have I really handed Danielle's care over to Him yet?"

Chapter 30

The Unopened Christmas Present

One morning when I went into Danielle's room, she was sleeping and I had difficulty trying to wake her up. I thought, "Oh, my goodness, now what?"

A few moments later her nurse came into the room and I asked him what was wrong with her. He said that he had given her morphine.

"For what?" I inquired.

His answer really upset me, "Because she was agitated and crying."

"Well," I asked, "Did you bother to check her brief?" (A brief is a sort of diaper used by the hospital for patients who are incontinent and thus unable to control their bladders and bowels.)

The nurse said he had checked the brief but only after he had given her the morphine. "Was her brief messy?" I asked.

When he said yes, I hissed at him, "That was all she needed then was her brief to be changed." Then I growled, "You write it on her chart that she is not to be given morphine until all other possibilities are ruled out. All she needed was a fresh brief and instead you gave her a drug. Was that the first and only thing you could think of?" He apologized, but I still was very upset.

Later, after the morphine had worn off, I decided to help Danielle get cleaned up. To clean her teeth I used sponge swabs that were made for that purpose. While I was using one of them on her teeth and mouth, the swab hit something in the back of her throat, so I pulled it. "Oh, no" I thought, "I just pulled her feeding tube." A female nurse came in at that moment and tried to help me. "I think it is hooked on her feeding tube." I explained and started pulling the swab forward. It wasn't the feeding tube at all. Instead it was a formation of brownish gunk that must have been built up from continually using the swabs to clean her mouth. Apparently the small amount of cleaner on the swab and her own saliva together made the accumulation which just grew larger and strung down her throat. The nurse and I cleaned it out. Afterward, I said to her, "No wonder she couldn't swallow right."

After her mouth was cleaned, Danielle continually wanted something to drink. At that time the doctors were only allowing her to have plain water until they conducted a swallow test. That would determine whether or not she could take food and liquids all right without choking on them. She frequently made grunting noises and blinked her eyes to tell me to put a few drops of water in her mouth. Every once in a while I also sneaked in a taste of juice as well.

Under the brief that Danielle had to wear, she developed a terrible rash that often bled. When she wet or messed herself it was very painful so she became agitated and cried. At that time the only way she could express herself was to cry, grunt or blink her eyes. I remember one time a nurse was there helping me change her brief and bedding. While we worked together she made the comment, "Oh, you're good at this. You must be used to it." I took her meaning to be that I was used to having a handicapped child. "No, Danielle was completely normal before we came here." I answered. The nurse was shocked. She asked what had happened. I explained the whole situation to her.

I was with Danielle the day of the physical therapist's first visit to her. She could move her arms and legs but not with controlled movements. The therapist's plan was to stretch her muscles in order to keep them flexible. I recall sitting on the couch in her room when two of the therapists started stretching both her arms and her legs. At that same moment a pastor walked in the room. He was from Vassar and had come to Ann Arbor to visit with us. After greeting me he asked how Danielle was doing. I don't know what came over me but, just at that instant it hit me that she was no longer normal. She had become physically handicapped and needed others to move her arms and legs for her. I had already known that, of course, but somehow it just hadn't sunk in.

"I'm sorry, Pastor, but I have to get out of here right now." I blurted and ran out the door and down the hallway to the elevator. After taking it down to the ground level and locating my car, I drove home and did not return that day.

"Am I going mad?" I asked myself. "It was only physical therapy."

I cried all the way home. Everything was bothering me. I even thought about the Christmas present that Mark and I had bought for Danielle. We had gotten her a television set that she couldn't even see. How sad and ironic that was.

Chapter 31

A Second Visit To The Intensive Care Unit

On New Years Day I decided to take Cole and Casey with me when I visited Danielle. I packed a bag for them and took the double stroller. At that time Cole was already two years old and Casey was only nine months old. Danielle was having a good day—she was starting to say a few words and was moving her arms and legs where she wanted them. However, she still had no control over her hands or fingers.

The neurologist asked Danielle a series of questions to test her memory. The first one he asked her was what day it was. She answered, "A couple of days before Christmas." I thought to myself, "Oh, That's right, she still doesn't know that she missed Christmas." The doctor continued asking her questions and she answered all of them correctly. She remembered her own name and her favorite music groups, she could count and say the alphabet, and she knew Cole's name and age correctly.

"Yes!" I exulted. That was great news. The neurologist left and I had to catch him and explain that it was my fault Danielle still thought that it was before Christmas.

Over the next few days the doctors did not discuss any further treatment for Danielle. They carefully watched her blood counts and kept close track of how much progress she was making in the other areas where there were problems. On January 4th still another complication appeared. She began experiencing seizures. The two of us were having a conversation in her room and suddenly she stopped talking and stared off into space. I called her name but it was as if I wasn't even there. I had already learned previously that was a sign of a seizure. "Danielle is having a seizure right now," I told her nurse after I found her in the hallway.

The neurologist decided that he wanted another test done on Danielle. They brought in a machine resembling a computer and placed small leads all over her head. Then they wrapped her head in gauze to keep the leads attached. Over the next few days the machine constantly read Danielle's brainwaves and reported all of her seizures, how long they lasted and how intense they were. The technician taught me to read the monitor and the printout so I could look for them myself. At the same time the doctor started Danielle on an anti-seizure medication. I hoped that the new problem would not be too much of a setback. I prayed, "Dear God, she was starting to do much better. Please let that continue."

During the next two days Danielle's seizures became more frequent and more intense. It got to the point that her brain was not getting any breaks from them. The neurologist came up with a plan. He explained to me that slowly he wanted to put her into a drug induced coma. He said that if her brain could go to sleep then the seizures would probably stop.

While Danielle was in the coma, she couldn't talk to me so I lay with her and held her hand. I hoped that she sensed I was there. Once, while I was lying there, she started to choke on her own tongue and saliva. I quickly pushed the call button and the nurse who responded called one of the hospital Alert Codes on her. After that crisis, the doctors decided that she would have to be moved back into the Intensive Care Unit for the duration of the coma because she was unable to control her muscles. Once Danielle was back in the ICU, she was placed on life support again. I wondered, "Why, why why? Why was she having such a serious setback?"

Danielle's ICU room was one of the glass cubicles and from there I could see into the other rooms. In the next room a large family was gathered around the bed. There were so many they were extending out into the hallway. I didn't know what was going on until a nurse asked me if I were bothered by the situation next door. Then I figured it out. The boy there was being taken off life support. He was going home to be with God.

I told her that it was okay, but that was not the truth. It did bother me, not because they all were gathered there, but because I wanted never to be in that situation. My heart went out to the family. I prayed fervently, "Please, God, I couldn't make that kind of decision. I couldn't watch Danielle suffer like that. Please don't ever make me do that." I must have repeated that about twenty times. Then I crawled in bed and lay next to Danielle for a while and sang our song to her. "Hold On For One More Day."

By January 8th the seizures had nearly stopped but there was still another problem. Danielle's white blood count had begun to drop. Up until then it had been climbing so the doctors wondered if the seizure medication were affecting it adversely. Everything was bothering me at that point and I wondered to myself, "It seems as though there is always something going wrong. Can't it just go forward smoothly, for once?"

The physical therapist made casts to put on Danielle's legs, feet and hands in order to keep the muscles stretched. Otherwise the muscles would shorten and become stiff and, therefore, useless. Though I knew they were there to help her, I hated seeing the casts as well as all the wires and tubes that were in her.

Each day I walked by a plaque hanging on the side wall of the hallway. On the plaque was a poem that a mother wrote about her son. I loved the poem because of what she said in it, but I felt bad for that mom. No author was indicated.

Know That I Am In Control

"If I lend to you for a little time
A child of mine," He said,
"For you to love while he lives
And mourn for when he's dead"

"It may be six or seven years,
Or twenty-two or three.
But, will you till I call him back
Take care of him for me?"

"He brought his charms to gladden you,
And though his stay was brief,
You'll have his lovely memories as
Solace for your grief."

"I could not promise he would stay
Since all from Earth return,
But, there were lessons taught down there
I wanted him to learn."

"I had looked the wide world over
In my search for teachers true,
And from the throngs that crowd the earth
I selected you.

"You did give him all your love,
Don't think the labor vain.
Don't hate me that I came to call
To take him back again."

I fancied that I heard you say,
"Dear Lord, Thy will be done."
For all the joy your son did bring,
The risk of grief was run."

"You sheltered him with tenderness,
You loved him every day,
And for the happiness you've known
Forever grateful stay."

"And though the angels called for him
Much sooner than you'd planned,
Know that I am in control,
And don't try to understand."

Most days were pretty much the same and there was little news that came my way. Though she couldn't hear me, in my loneliness I talked to Danielle, "Everything is staying the same. You are still in ICU. I feel really lonely when you are here. Most days I come to the hospital by myself so there is no one to talk to. I can't even bring Cole and Casey along when you are here. Please wake up soon. I miss you so much."

Chapter 32

Progress

The story was "more of the same" through the middle of January. Danielle remained in the coma and so it was impossible to talk with her. Because she was in the Intensive Care Unit, most of the time I had to visit her alone. Cole and Casey were not allowed in that unit. Though the hospital staff was very friendly, it was not the same as if I had been able to talk with family, especially the children. The days and weeks seemed to go on forever.

Over the next few days Danielle began to show some signs of improvement. She had fewer seizures so the doctors could take away the respirator and they moved her out of the Intensive Care Unit and into a regular room. At the time her eyesight was extremely poor and they were not at all certain how much of it she would ever get back again. We communicated in very basic ways with Danielle either sticking out her tongue or blinking her eyes to tell me things.

Danielle still had the feeding tube in her nose until January 24th when she was given a swallow test. The purpose of the test was to determine if she could get food down without choking on it. She was given a thick, chalky substance to swallow. While she was doing that they took pictures in order to see if it were going down her throat and not into her lungs. The results of that test were excellent. She was able to swallow perfectly and so the doctors could remove the feeding tube. That was a huge blessing to me.

About the same time as the swallow test, Danielle had another bone marrow biopsy. I mentioned to the doctor that she recently had a biopsy in Detroit and asked him if he could compare the results of the two tests. He said that he would try to get a copy of the earlier test results in order to do that.

At the time I was getting confusing reports from the various hospital personnel. One therapist suggested that Danielle would never walk or talk again. She felt that Danielle would likely remain close to the same state she was in at the time. I refused to believe that. Lying in a bed and not being able to move was not Danielle. I was certain that her spirit would not tolerate that. She had progressed so much over the last few weeks that she had started talking to me again. The words came slow at first, but she seemed to progress quickly.

Yet another subject was brought up at about the same time. That was that the doctors discussed doing surgery on Danielle's lung in order to remove the lobe with the pneumonia lesion. No decision had been made about when the operation would take place, but they were preparing for it and suggested that I do the same.

Through the early days of February our life fell into a routine. Each day I took Cole and Casey and we spent the day at the hospital. We either stayed in Danielle's room or I put the babies in the double stroller and Danielle in a wheel chair and we traveled throughout the hospital. I noticed that some people were amazed when they saw me coming down the hallway pushing the stroller with one hand and the wheel chair with the other. Often they made comments such as, "I don't know how you do it." Each time I replied, "You have to do what you have to do. If it were you, then you would be able to do it, too."

Sometimes when I really thought about it, I did have some guilt concerning Casey. I realized that during her first year of life she had practically been raised in a hospital. It must have been an unstable environment for her. I didn't worry about Cole because he was always very flexible and easy-going. Perhaps I should not have let such fears bother me—after all we were all together and that was what really counted.

Chapter 33

Lung Surgery

Over the next couple of weeks Danielle's condition made improvements by leaps and bounds. She could talk in sentences and could move her arms and legs where she wanted them to go. She still couldn't do detail work with her fingers, but the hospital staff was working on that, too.

The doctor made the decision to do the lung surgery and scheduled it for February 6th. He took the time to explain the procedure to me. He told me the right lung has three lobes and the left has only two. They would remove the top lobe of the right lung where the infection was located. I asked why they couldn't remove just the ball of pnuemonia itself, but he insisted that the entire lobe would have to go.

I stayed overnight with Danielle before the operation. The next day, just before 8 a.m., the surgical team came into her room to take her down to the surgery wing. They wheeled her in the hospital bed through the hallway and stopped just outside big double doors with a sign that read Operating Room (OR). We had to wait there until they were ready to take her in.

The thought of the surgery frightened me badly. In the back of my mind I could still hear the voice of the surgeon from Hurley Hospital telling me that Danielle had only a fifty percent chance of making it through this operation. The Ann Arbor surgeons, however, felt that she had strength enough to endure it. I just had to have faith. She had battled through so much already and so I, too, felt that she was strong enough to go through it.

In the hallway outside the operating room, I sat on the side of Danielle's bed and we talked. She was nervous and said, "Mom, I'm scared! Is it going to be okay?"

I replied in the affirmative, "Yes, Boo, these doctors know that you are strong enough to have the surgery. If you weren't then they wouldn't put you through it right now."

The nurse came out and said that I could go into the operating room with Danielle and would be able to stay until she was put under. That news made both of us feel a little better. To enter the operating room, though, I had to wear a suit that made me look like an astronaut. I donned the outfit in the dressing room and again went outside to wait with Danielle. In an attempt to get both of us through the wait I said, "Boo, I wish you could see me right now so that you could have a good laugh. I look like an astronaut. I have a suit on over my clothing, covers over my shoes, a headpiece over my hair and a face mask." As I explained my outfit to her, she sort of giggled.

Finally they wheeled her into the operating room. Where they moved her from the hospital bed onto a very narrow one. I thought, "Oh, my goodness, she'll fall off!" Next they hooked up all the machines and lines that were going to be used. I was in awe of everything they did. In a very short time I heard the doctor call to her, "Danielle, Danielle." He turned to me saying, "Okay, Mom, she's asleep. Give her a kiss because it's time to say goodbye." I bent over and kissed her cheek but was thinking, "No! You didn't give me time to say anything to her. That was too fast. I didn't get to tell her that I loved her!"

I fled to the dressing room with tears streaming down my face. As quickly as I could, I peeled off the protective suit. The receptionist asked, "Are you all right? I can show you where you go to wait." Instead of answering her, I ran out of the room. I needed a few moments to myself before joining our family members and friends in the waiting room. Up until then, when serious things occurred, I didn't have time to think about them before they happened. With this surgery, however, I knew what could happen and what could go wrong. Also, this time I knew her chances for survival.

In the waiting room I found my Grandmother Summerfield, my Uncle Randy, Vi Faiver (my neighbor), our pastor and Mark. My neighbor, Vi, was a wonderful lady. She had come to the hospital for the surgery and planned to stay the night with Danielle so that I could leave. I hadn't seen Cole and Casey for a couple of days, so Vi insisted that I go home and take a break from the hospital.

Seeing Vi there made me think about some of the different people who had helped out during Danielle's many stays in the hospital. My sister, Alisha, always took care of Cole and Casey on a moment's notice. My Uncle Lee and Aunt Leora Stedry often drove my grandmother to the hospital while Danielle was in the Intensive Care Unit so she could be with us. My father-in-law and his lady friend occasionally stayed the night with Danielle and would sleep sitting in the rocking chairs. I'm so grateful for the help that everyone gave us.

During the surgery we received several updates on its progress. The operation began at 8 a.m. and about 11a.m. the surgeon came out and said that it was nearly over and she was doing well. He had already dissected the lung tissue that had been removed and it looked as though they had taken out all the infection. He also mentioned that he was replacing her old port that had been ruined in the Intensive Care Unit. He explained further that they were going to put in the other type of port that hangs out the chest in front. I objected and said, "No, you're not. I want the same type of port that she already had. That way we don't have to worry so much about infection and Danielle will be able to take baths and go swimming." He agreed to do that. The doctor took me into the back room to give me more details about the operation. He drew a picture of her lung. It showed the top lobe missing. He went on to explain how they were trying to save the rest of it.

It was a real relief to know that the hardest part of the surgery was over. I went back to the waiting room again and soon realized that all of us were getting hungry. By that time I was relaxed about the rest of the operation so I went down to Wendy's Restaurant, next to the cafeteria, and got salads and took them back to the waiting room for everyone to eat.

At 1:30 that afternoon, a nurse came out of the operating room to tell us that Danielle was in the recovery room. She said I wouldn't be able to see her until she started to wake up from the anesthesia. By 4 p.m. I began to get nervous that something was wrong because it was taking so long. Finally, someone informed me that they were moving her directly to the Intensive Care Unit and that I could go up and meet her. As I made my way there, I thought about it being her third trip to the ICU, but this time she shouldn't have to stay very long. They just needed to monitor her lung for a few hours.

Once Danielle was settled in the Intensive Care Unit, the doctor explained the morphine drip that they had attached to her. In case the pain got really bad and she needed it, I could push a button which would send a bolus (a large amount) of the morphine into her body— but only at certain specified intervals. The doctor also placed a very fine tube through the incision near the lung so that the morphine could go directly where the pain was located. At the time she was comfortably sedated and I wanted to be next to her so I carefully climbed into the bed with her.

Chapter 34

A Second Lung Surgery

The next morning, which was February seventh, the doctors decided to move Danielle from the Intensive Care Unit to a regular room. She was awake and wanted the respirator removed. She also seemed to be in more pain so I had to push the morphine button for the bolus as soon as the allotted time has passed. I tried to comfort her as much as I could but she didn't seem to be getting any relief from the pain.

By February 8th she was having extreme pain. She kept her body completely still and begged to have the button pushed. I timed the intervals so that I could push it as soon as possible, but it didn't seem to be touching the discomfort she was experiencing. The surgeon came to check on her and when he realized how much pain she was in, he ordered an x-ray of her lung. I tried to comfort her by rubbing her arm, but she whispered, "Mom, don't touch me. It hurts even if you just touch me!" That really tore me up inside. I couldn't stand seeing my baby in so much agony.

The x-ray results showed that there was a fluid buildup in the space around Danielle's lungs and that the middle lobe had collapsed. During surgery they had inserted a chest tube on the right side of her lung that was supposed to keep the lung inflated but it wasn't doing its job. The surgeon decided to take her back to the OR and move the chest tube to a different area in order to see if it would re-inflate the middle lobe.

Once more Danielle was taken to the OR and I went back to the waiting room. I hated the waiting game of not knowing what was going on. Again I stayed there all day, but this time all by myself. No one came out to update me or to let me know when she was in the recovery room. Finally, I was the last person left in the waiting room so I lay across three chairs to try to rest. The stress had totally exhausted me. I kept hoping that the second surgery would correct the problem. As far as I was concerned I was getting just too familiar with the Intensive Care Unit and the staff there.

By 6 p.m. I had enough waiting. I picked up the phone on the waiting room desk and dialed the recovery room extension. I was desperate for information and said, "This is Danielle's mom. I have been here all day and have not heard anything. Is everything all right?" The nurse hastily responded, "I'll have someone come out to speak with you in just a moment."

That sent me into a panic. "Oh, no," I thought, "Something has happened. If it wasn't bad, then the nurse would have just told me rather than sending someone to talk to me. What happened? Not again. Not something terrible again. Danielle was just starting to come back from the last battle. She was recovering better than they expected—her memory was pretty much intact and she was talking in full sentences. She still couldn't see and didn't have complete control of her body but she could beat those problems, too." My thoughts ran away with me because of my panic.

The doctor interrupted my frantic thoughts by saying, "Mrs. Tausch?" After I responded, he said, "I'm sorry. I thought you knew that we moved Danielle right up to the Intensive Care Unit for the night and that you could meet her there." What a relief! As I hurried out on my way to the ICU, I called back to him, "No, I didn't know that, but thank you!"

Once I got to the unit I asked the nurse how long Danielle had been there. "A couple of hours," she answered, "I had to mark on the chart that there were no parents or anyone else with her."

"Oh, no, I've been with her all day but they forgot to tell me in the OR waiting room that she was coming here, so I have been sitting there all day just waiting," I said.

The nurse apologized for the mix-up. That didn't matter then— nothing did. Danielle was there and looked as though she was resting well. That was all that really mattered.

By the next day, February 9th, Danielle's lung showed no improvement. Silently I screamed, "How much longer can she take that kind of constant pain?"

Because Mark had been spending time at home taking care of Cole and Casey, he wanted to be with Danielle for a while. The next day he went to the hospital and I stayed at home. That day the surgeon decided to perform a second lung surgery in order to remove the middle lobe. Mark stayed in the waiting room during that operation because I wasn't able to go to the hospital until he came home to be with the babies. Like the other, this surgery also made me very nervous, but I was comforted by the fact that Mark was there and also I had confidence in the surgeon.

The operation went very well. Mark came home and I went in to see Danielle. I could see immediately that the second one had made a big improvement in her condition. The pain was almost completely gone and she no longer asked for the bolus of morphine. That was a big relief for me as well.

Once I was able to collect myself and thought about how much of Danielle's lung was missing, I had a number of questions for the doctor. I wanted to know such things as: Could she fly in an airplane? Could she play sports? Will she feel out of breath all the time? The list went on and on. The doctor answered my questions as well as he could.

Chapter 35

The Scar

On February 13th Danielle once again was moved from the Intensive Care Unit to another room in the hospital. The doctors felt that she was then well enough so that she could resume the physical therapy. Two nurses came into her room to get her out of bed so that she could sit up in a reclining chair for a while. To do that one of them lifted her legs and the other lifted under her arms. I noticed that when the nurse lifted her, Danielle winced in pain.

"Watch it." I yelled, "She just had surgery. Don't you know that? You're one of those taking care of her and you don't even know she just had surgery? You may have ripped the incision open because it is just under her arm in the ribcage area."

The nurse apologized but that didn't do any good. I thought that it should be the hospital's policy that any staff member working on patients should first read the patient's chart so they were better informed.

I had begun learning the stretch exercises for physical therapy so that I could also help with taking care of Danielle. We were told that if her muscles were allowed to tighten and stiffen, the condition might not be reversible.

Up to then I hadn't looked at Danielle's surgery scar because I didn't know if I could handle seeing it. I wanted to look at it but was scared to. A day or two later I decided that I <u>had</u> to look at it. After all, I would have to see it when I helped take care of her so I thought that I should get my first sight of it over with.

Carefully I pulled Danielle's hospital gown back and took a peek. I do not know how to describe my feelings when I first saw the scar. It really made me sick to my stomach. That was not because of how it looked, but rather because it was a symbol of everything that she had been through. I touched the tips of my fingers to the edge of the scar and immediately got goose bumps. It was very long, beginning about two inches from her spine and following her ribs horizontally around to her front where it stopped just before her breast bone. In addition there were two or three circular scars from the chest tubes in various places on her body.

Because of her temporary blindness, Danielle could not see her own scar but would someday be able to. When that day came, I would not want her to see herself as ugly because of the changes in her body. I wanted to encourage her to have only positive thoughts about it. Most people say that beauty is only skin deep, but I know that a teenager does not see it that way. I wanted her to look at her scar and be proud of it. In the future when life was getting her down and she felt overwhelmed, I hoped that she would think to herself, "At the time I earned this scar, I fought my hardest battle and won. I can get through anything now."

The scar would be a symbol of Danielle's past, present and future. It represented her will and strength in the past, whatever battle she was going through at the present time, and her strength and determination to survive any problems in the future. Every time I look at it, I would be strengthened also.

Chapter 36

Playing Dress Up

I often wondered how much more Danielle would have to weather. She was only eleven years old and had already endured more than anyone I knew. She still hadn't won the battle with the aplastic anemia and had to continue that fight. The doctor suggested beginning a new treatment. He was concerned that because of the trauma Danielle had gone through, her bone marrow recovery may have suffered a setback. I wasn't convinced that she was ready for another treatment at the time.

After two straight months in the hospital, there was little talk about Danielle coming home. When it was brought up, the doctors always mentioned that certain special requirements had to be met before she would be allowed to go home with me. She would have to be able to use the potty or a bedside commode and she hadn't attempted either at that time. Also, I had to be able to get her in and out of the shower. In addition, Danielle would have to be eating better. Finally, therapy for her had to be located closer to our home.

One day I took Danielle, Cole and Casey down to the hospital play center to find something to do that was fun for that day's therapy. In the play room they had a wooden tower with all kinds of play clothes hung on it. I remembered how much Danielle loved playing dress up as a little girl. To me, play is the best kind of therapy. We spent some time there and had fun putting a hat on her head and a feather scarf around her neck. We added a little jewelry that made her look very fancy. By that time Danielle's hair had grown out a couple of inches and it was very curly. I made the comment to her, "Boo, I think you over-wished this time. You got double what you wanted, because your hair is very curly."

I took pictures of Danielle in the dress up outfit. Every time that she did something new, I got out the camera or the camcorder; I was starting to get quite a collection of pictures of her taken in different places in the hospital.

At the play center, the woman who was in charge most days, asked Danielle if she would like to have a song made up just about her. That was exciting to Danielle because she loved music. We filled out some forms which asked about her life and the things she loved best. Then the forms were sent to a music studio where an artist would make up the song using the information on the forms. Danielle was even able to pick out what kind of music it would be and she chose soft rock. We were told that she would probably have to wait about two weeks for the CD. We both thought it would be very interesting to hear her very own song when it was finished.

Even though Danielle still was hindered by the feeding tube in her nose, her determination to do things on her own became much stronger. Over the last couple of weeks she had improved by leaps and bounds in therapy. Most days she cooperated with the therapists, but there were days when she did not feel like doing what they wanted and she could be very stubborn. I saw that stubbornness as a blessing because it told me that when Danielle put her mind to do something, she was going to do it. On the negative side, I noticed that she had regressed a little in maturity, but on the other hand her long term memory was left intact. Some news was good and some was not so good.

One day when I walked into Danielle's room she exclaimed, "Mom, you have a red shirt on!" I could not believe what I had just heard. She went on to explain that she was starting to see different colors but still could not make out objects. If she could see that well, then it was a huge blessing. I thought to myself, "She is going to be all right. I just know it!"

I finally did have to tell Danielle that she had missed Christmas. She was very upset about it but, to make her feel better, I promised when she came home that we would set the tree up and have Christmas all over again. She was happy with that.

Regularly, I asked the nurses what medicines were being given to Danielle because I wanted to know about everything that was going on with her. February 25th happened to be one of the days that I asked about the meds. When the nurse named them I noticed that one of them was cyclosporine. I demanded to know when the new drug had been added to those she took. The nurse replied that it was three days before. I told her that the doctor and I had only talked about it briefly and I hadn't given my permission for it to be used. The nurse arranged for me to discuss it with the doctor and during our talk he convinced me that Danielle should continue taking the cyclosporine.

In the therapy sessions, Danielle began standing while holding on to something solid. That improvement made my heart soar; since I had been told that she might never either walk or talk again. Oh, how I wanted her to prove all of them wrong. I wanted her to succeed. Her balance still was not very good because she had to hang on to something, but just the fact that she was standing was unbelievable. The doctors even started to speak about Danielle's release sometime in the future. Of course, she had to meet the requirements first. Meanwhile, she stayed there and had three therapies three times a day.

The therapists put together a special telephone for Danielle to use. Because she did not have full control of her hands and couldn't see well, she couldn't use a regular phone. They hooked a big red button to her bedside. When the phone rang she could hit the button with her arm. That turned on the speaker phone so that she could talk to and also hear the other person. One particular night when I called her, she had a roommate. She seemed particularly lonely so I sang our song and she sang with me. The other patient's family probably thought I was crazy because they were able to hear me over the speaker. But I didn't care, I just wanted Danielle to feel better.

About that time I started putting Danielle in a regular wheelchair, instead of the specially made one. She was doing much better and needed the added exercise. In the regular wheelchair she wrapped her arms around the arms of the chair, leaned forward and pushed her feet against the floor to move. At first she could only push the chair backward, but, after a while, she learned to propel it forward, too.

Danielle's sight progressed to where she could distinguish more colors but she still couldn't describe what she was able to see. To understand it better, I would question her. I asked if it were all mixed up, or if she saw like a fly (many pictures at one time). Her answer was always the same, "I don't know how to describe it."

I knew that Danielle's body movements and sight would never again be one hundred percent but it was amazing how far she had come already. How far she could improve in the future was a question that no one could answer at that time.

Chapter 37

Getting Ready To Come Home

On St. Patrick's Day I decided that Danielle should attempt to use the bedside commode and try to take a shower. She still needed to work on both those tasks before she would be able to come home. Those turned out to be much easier than I had thought they would be. Probably the challenge that was the hardest to accomplish was for Danielle to consume 1800 calories a day. That was a goal that she hadn't come near at the time.

After Danielle showered, I took her, Cole and Casey for a stroll around the hospital. Down in the lobby where I always entered, they had a game carnival set up for the patients. Danielle played the games and won beanie babies as prizes. It was perfect therapy because while playing the games she had to throw balls and reach for things. She had so much fun that it didn't seem like therapy at all. While I watched Danielle enjoying herself, I thought that if a child must be in a hospital, then that was the best one to be in. I loved that place. They tried to make it fun for sick children and, even though it was a large hospital, they were very family oriented.

Finally, the day I was waiting for came on March 5ᵗʰ when Danielle took a couple of baby steps with a walker. I don't know when I have ever been so proud and so happy for her. She had conquered it all. She improved so much in therapy that she showed everyone she could make a great comeback. The human body, especially a child's body, can make amazing recoveries. I still had to push Cole and Casey in the stroller and pull Danielle in a wheelchair, but I didn't think that would last long.

With her first steps, Danielle had trouble with the heavy gray walker the therapist had given her to use. To help that situation, I asked them to order one with wheels so she wouldn't have to lift it for each step she took. To pay for the new walker we used some of the donated money from the fundraisers. What a blessing it was to have the money available in our time of need. I described to Danielle the various colors that the walker came in and she chose candy apple red.

At the beginning of April Danielle was still in the hospital. The doctors finally were able to arrange for out-patient therapy closer to Vassar so that I could take her home. That was both exciting and yet scary for me. It made me nervous because I would have total charge of her care when she left the hospital. It felt like when she was born and I brought her home for the very first time. Danielle and two small babies, Cole and Casey, all would be totally dependent on me and I wondered if I could do it.

I could not help being a little angry when I wondered why so many of Danielle's problems happened just when her bone marrow was starting to heal. I really thought that she had beaten the disease. Another thing that made me angry was that Danielle, for a long time, wanted a little brother or sister and was very excited when they came along. But once she did have them in her life, she couldn't even enjoy them.

Mulling over my anger about all of Danielle's problems made me think back to the night just before Christmas when she was brought in to the hospital. By then I had learned the reason the ambulance took so long to get to us. It was because the 911 operator made a serious blunder and paged the firemen instead of an ambulance. My brother-in-law, a local fireman was the one who returned the operator's call and said, "You have a child coughing up blood coming across our pagers. You need to page an ambulance instead of us."

When I heard that news I was furious. That night I had called 911 twice because it took so long for the ambulance to get there. It made matters even worse when I found out the delay was merely because the operator paged the wrong people.

I had clearly told the operator that Danielle was coughing up blood; so how could she get that wrong? Her mistake nearly cost Danielle's life. If she had gotten to the hospital twenty minutes earlier and had received platelets that much sooner, all of this might not have happened.

Later, I was so angry about the blunder that I called a lawyer because I wanted something done about it. The lawyer explained to me that there is a law preventing 911 operators from being sued. So, what it comes down to is this: we pay their salaries through our taxes or on our phone bills but, even if they screw up in the worst possible way, as that one did, there is absolutely nothing we can do about it. That is just not fair!

Chapter 38

Coming Home

Danielle was released from the Ann Arbor hospital near the end of April and I had to buy a van to bring her wheelchair and other things home. The specially made wheelchair wouldn't fit easily into the van because it was heavy and wouldn't fold, so I marched it back to the therapy unit where we had gotten it and left it there. After we were home I borrowed a regular wheelchair from a local church and she used that. I knew that the special chair wasn't really necessary because Danielle could move around in a regular one and she could use her new walker.

On our way home from Ann Arbor, Danielle said that she really would like to see Cindy and the other nurses at Hurley Hospital in Flint. Since it was not far out of our way, I decided that we could go there. I didn't want to disappoint her because that was her first time outside hospital walls in three months. I also wondered what the nurses would think of Danielle at that time. The last time they saw her she was a normal pre-teen girl; since then the brain damage had changed her appearance somewhat.

Danielle could not go long distances with her walker so I wheeled her up to the second floor. It seemed strange going into Hurley Hospital again, and yet, in an eerie way, it was comforting too. We went through the double doors into the Pediatrics Unit to the nurse's desk and all the nurses gathered around Danielle. Cindy was there and the first thing she did was grab Danielle and give her a huge hug. It was very emotional.

Out of Danielle's hearing I confessed to Cindy, "I'm scared. I'm not sure how I'll handle having three children so dependent on me." Her answer was short but right on target, "Just be thankful that you have three instead of two." She was right. I was so busy worrying about taking care of Danielle outside the hospital that I forgot to be thankful about that.

After a short visit, we were back on the road toward home. When we got there, we had Christmas all over again like I had promised Danielle. She wanted to see her bedroom because it had been a long time since she was able to do "girly things" in her own space. Mark carried her upstairs and sat her on the bed so she could feel as if she really was at home.

We soon fell back into the routine of making daily trips. We alternated between going to therapy in Flint, about forty-five minutes away, and to the clinic in Ann Arbor, which was further. There was something to do every day. Danielle made real progress with the therapy but her eyesight still was not very good.

Part of Danielle's daily medications included injections that I gave her and taking six to eight large cyclosporine pills. The doctors were trying to maintain a certain level of the drug in her body, but the pills made her sick and she often threw them up. One day when we were talking with the doctor at the clinic, I asked him if cyclosporine came in any form other than pills. He told me that it could be taken in a concentrated liquid. When we tried that, it stayed in Danielle's stomach a little better but she had a hard time swallowing it. It smelled awful and tasted worse. At first I tried mixing it with Kool-Aid or juice, but she preferred taking the dose and then chasing it with the Kool-Aid or juice.

Chapter 39

Mother And Daughters Conversations

Danielle and I had a lot of good conversations while we were on the way to therapy or to the clinic at the hospital. Talking helped to pass the many hours we spent on the road.

Once she shocked me when she said, "Mom, I'm not important, am I?"

"What makes you say that?" I wanted to know.

She responded with, "Because you have Cole and Casey, and Mark is their dad, so I don't fit in."

"Oh, no, Boo, you fit in. You were my first baby and that alone makes you very special. When a new mom has a baby that is when she experiences the miracle of birth for the first time. It's unforgettable."

I was aware that Danielle was changed both physically and mentally, but I wanted to know how she viewed herself and if she felt that all she had been through made her a different person. So, one day I asked her, "Boo, do you still feel the same inside or do you feel as though you have changed since the accident?" (That is what I now call it.)

She answered, "No, Mom, I'm still the same." And I thought, "Yes, you are!"

Danielle continued to have a problem with nausea from her medications. She was very thin because of her difficulty with keeping food down. Sometimes on the way to therapy she was sick in the van. When that happened I would drive the rest of the way to the office in order to tell them that she was ill and wouldn't be in that day. Then we would turn around to come home again.

When she was having an especially good day, Danielle would walk a little way with her walker and then let go of it and stand for a minute or two on her own. Her balance still was not very good, but other than that she was doing great.

One day the therapist asked Danielle to take a step without the walker or any other support. She was afraid to do it and became upset. I was watching the therapy that particular day and, like Danielle, was a little nervous about it. I didn't say anything at the time because I figured the therapist knew what she was doing. She stood Danielle up and coaxed her into letting go by saying, "Nothing is going to happen because if you start to fall, I'll catch you." Danielle finally agreed to try because the therapist was not going to give up until she did.

The therapist let go of Danielle and stepped back. She asked her to take one step toward her outstretched arms. Danielle raised her arms and attempted to lift her foot but when she did that she lost her balance. Instead of falling forward, she fell backward landing on her back and striking her head on the floor.

I could tell that the therapist felt very bad but that didn't help any. I was furious. Didn't she understand what a simple fall like that could do to Danielle? Her blood did not clot well and a fall could cause internal bleeding. I let the therapist know that I wasn't happy about what had happened. I also felt that I shouldn't have to explain to her how easily

Danielle could have been seriously hurt. For the next couple of hours I was on pins and needles as I waited and watched for Danielle to show any symptoms that could indicate more internal bleeding. Thankfully none appeared.

One day in the van on the way to therapy, a thought came to me. Something inside of me said, "Reach over and touch Danielle's hand." So I did. Next I thought, "Study the hand. Etch the look and feel of it in your mind." It seemed so tiny and fragile to me. That soft, small hand was like a symbol of Danielle's body which had battled bravely for a very long time. Would we ever reach recovery?

Chapter 40

The Last Attempt At Treatment

The clinic in Ann Arbor was very child oriented. Along one wall were reclining chairs where the patients could either take a nap or play video games on the television/VCR that sat by each chair. In the middle of the room were all sorts of toys as well as a craft table in case they were interested in that type of activity. Danielle and I did some of the crafts together while she was there. Dr. Williams was her doctor in the clinic. He was a very nice man and Danielle really liked him.

Dr. Williams decided to start another treatment in an attempt to cure Danielle's aplastic anemia. The therapy was the rabbit serum (ALG) that had been offered in Detroit when we had chosen the chemotherapy instead. He didn't really give me a choice that time, because when I hesitated about giving my approval, he said, "Look, her bone marrow is not recovering. Because of her recent trauma, its recovery may even have had a setback. It has now been just short of a year since she was diagnosed and we have to try something else." So, I agreed to the treatment. The doctor gave Danielle the choice of either starting in a couple of days or waiting until the following Monday. Of course she chose to wait until Monday. Who could blame her? She had only been out of the hospital a few weeks.

The weekend came and went and so did May 16ᵗʰ. Danielle remembered that was the day one year ago when she had been diagnosed with the disease.

At the time when Danielle came home from Ann Arbor, we made a bedroom for her in the living room because she could not go up the stairs to her own room. We tried to make it her own space as well as we could by setting up a mattress, her own television and also her dresser in the corner. Often I made a bed on the living room floor to be near her in case she needed anything during the night.

The Sunday night before the treatment was to start, I decided that Cole, Casey and I would all sleep there so that we all were together in the same room. I got Danielle ready for bed and started to transfer her from the wheelchair. While she was standing, I wrapped my arms around her and hugged. I said, "I don't know what I would have done if I had lost you, Boo."

"I know, Mom." She answered. We stood there hugging one another for a few moments. I just wanted to feel her close to me.

Then I couldn't get to sleep. I wasn't sure what caused me to lie there awake but I had a lot on my mind. It may have been the one year anniversary of the diagnosis or new stress about the upcoming treatment. I decided to talk to God about everything. That night I told Him that Danielle was His daughter, not mine. I gave her back to Him. I said, "God, she's Yours; you take care of her because You can heal her and I can't. I'm giving her to You, God, and Your will be done." I meant it from the bottom of my heart.

I felt something special during that prayer. I felt that God heard me and knew that I really meant what I said. Even though my battle was mental and not physical, I just couldn't do it alone any longer. Not when I also had Cole and Casey who were so dependent on me as well. I think <u>that</u> was what God was waiting for—for me to say that I needed Him and His help and that I couldn't do it alone.

Monday I checked Danielle into the hospital in Ann Arbor again. While that was going on, I thought of something and said to her, "You were granted a wish from the Make A Wish Foundation that you haven't used yet. When you get through this one week of treatment; we are going. No more putting it off. We'll find a place in Florida to have your blood counts taken and to receive your transfusions." She was very excited about that and, because I was, too, we talked about it for quite a while.

The new treatment was exceptional. I visited Danielle every day and called her each night and saw firsthand that Dr. Williams was happy that everything seemed to be going well. Her blood counts showed a small steady gain and she appeared to have no side effects from the therapy. Actually, I now think they were going too well.

The obvious ease and effectiveness of that ALG therapy caused me to feel guilty for choosing the chemotherapy in Detroit. What did I do? What was I thinking? It had made her very sick and even eventually caused her to become handicapped, and it was all my fault. I chose the wrong treatment. How could I have made such a huge mistake? It had almost cost Danielle her life. I was her mother and I was supposed to protect her, not put danger in her way.

Danielle was scheduled to come home the next Friday. That morning I called her to say that I would come to pick her up near her release time because I had some things to do at home first. She hadn't seen the doctor when I called so I told her I would phone later when she knew her checkout time.

That afternoon I called again and Danielle complained about a terrible headache. In fact it was so bad that the nurse gave her a prescription drug to help ease the pain. Then I talked to the nurse who informed me that she could not come home until the next day because of the headache. Danielle was crushed and began to cry. I told her that it was only one more night, just like our song says. I tried to help by saying, "Turn all the lights and TV off, lie back and try to relax." "Maybe the headache was from the ALG, so give the pain medicine time to do its work." I added.

I mentioned that I would come to the hospital later because first I needed to go to the grocery store and to get some things done before leaving. By then it was late afternoon and Cole and Casey were napping. I told Mark that I would go to the store while they were asleep and then I left.

Chapter 41

The Final Goodbye

I was only in the grocery store for about twenty minutes. I came down an aisle that faced the front of the store and, as I rounded the corner to go up the other, Mark was standing there with Cole and Casey. Cole stood beside him looking very sleepy and Casey was asleep in his arms. My stomach felt sick all of a sudden and my heart lurched. I knew something was wrong. Mark said, "Go! Get to the hospital now! Danielle's bleeding in her brain and they don't know if she'll last until you get there!"

After I raced the two blocks home, I called my mom and said, "I have to go now!" Mom was at our house in about two minutes and insisted on going with me. On our way to the hospital my thoughts were a jumble. "Please, God, let me make it in time." "I know that she will be okay." "She already had to battle a bleed once before and it turned out all right." Everything seemed so unreal to me.

When I got to the hospital the ICU doctors, along with Dr. Williams, talked with us. They explained that after looking at all the tests that had been run, there was nothing more they could do to help Danielle. The bleeding had shifted her brain off the brainstem and she would eventually be pronounced brain dead. If she did live, it would be in a vegetative condition.

They went on to explain that it would be our call as to when Danielle was taken off the life support and we could be with her as long as we wished. So far she was only showing one or two of the signs that indicate when a patient is brain dead. For instance, she was breathing above the ventilator which meant that she was breathing on her own. Because of that, I just couldn't accept all I had been told. Apparently I was in denial because she had an earlier close call and had made it through. So, I wondered, why couldn't she do the same this time?

Because I wanted to be with Danielle for a little while, I walked down to her room. For a few moments I needed a break from all that was being said. There was a male nurse attending to her and he asked if there were anything he could do for me.

"Yes, could you help me move all these wires so I can lie with her?"

His response was, "I haven't taken care of Danielle before, but I have heard of you. You are the mom who likes to lie with her daughter."

A bag of platelets was hanging on the IV pole so I asked the nurse, "If all they say is true, then why are you giving her platelets? Another child may need them."

I remembered back at Hurley Hospital there were some days when Danielle waited hours for platelets because there was a shortage of them. He didn't answer. I don't think that anyone knew what to say. I wondered, "Why did I say that?" I think it was because I was so angry at the time.

While lying there beside Danielle, I thought that it didn't feel any different than it had all the other times. It didn't feel as though she had left me. It felt exactly like when she was in the ICU before, and it seemed as though she should be coming out of it in a little while. I was not being realistic; I did not want to be.

Sometime during the middle of the night, I became so overwhelmed with everything that I needed to get out of there for a while. What I really felt like doing was running away. I thought, "Is she really not coming back this time? I can't take her off the respirator when she is breathing on her own. She is still fighting to stay alive. Why didn't God make the decision for me and just take her?" I was still hoping that the doctors were wrong.

Mom and I went back to Vassar. At home I lay between Cole and Casey and wondered how all of that could happen. I prayed for an answer. "God, I asked you to never put me in the situation where I had to make that kind of decision. I can't do that. I can't watch Danielle go." (I couldn't even say the word "die.") It was almost as if I were transported back to that ICU room and to the moment when I watched the family say goodbye to their little boy. Danielle was in that exact room he was in when his family said goodbye. "God, aren't you listening to me? Why are you doing this?"

My pastor came to our house very early the next morning to pray with me and to comfort me. I had a lot of questions for him, "If I make this decision, will God think that I killed Danielle? Why didn't God just take her so I didn't have to make the decision? Why did she have to go through a year of suffering, and having her hopes dashed to the ground, just to lose in the end anyway?" He didn't have the answers either.

Alisha, my sister came over that morning and asked to go to the hospital with me because she wanted to see Danielle again. I said to her, "You know what I have to do. Right?" She responded, "Yes." Then I asked, "Are you sure you want to be there?" She answered by insisting that she had to see Danielle again and even offered to drive me back to the hospital.

While on the way there, I had my cell phone with me and talked to Danielle's doctor. I told him that I couldn't do it, that I couldn't be there to watch her go. I said, "This is wrong. I'm her mom. I'm supposed to fix her and make her feel better." He said that would be all right but another doctor had to call me back to confirm that I was giving them permission to take her off life support.

I asked Alisha to turn the truck around because I couldn't go through with it. I wanted to go back home. Suddenly memories came flooding back about Danielle's last year. The main thing I remembered was promising when she was first diagnosed that I would be with her through everything. About five minutes later I said to Alisha, "I'm sorry. Could you turn us around again? I promised Boo that I would be there with her. I was there the day she was born and took her first breath and I need to be there when she takes her last." She did what I asked and got us back on the highway heading toward the hospital again. Just then my cell phone rang. It was the other doctor confirming that I had given permission to remove the life support. I told him that I had given permission but that I had changed my mind about being there and that I was on the way then. He said that they were going to wait for me.

When we got to the hospital, I climbed on the bed with Danielle and rubbed her stomach. My heart was breaking, I cried, "Boo, when you see the angels you take their hands and fly away home with them." Just then her knee jerked toward me and the heart rate machine began beeping because her rate jumped. That brought the nurse in to see what was happening. She exclaimed, "Danielle has been quiet all night. Not one thing happened until now." "Is that a sign that she knows

I'm here?" I wondered, "In case she does know, is she trying to tell me something?"

I asked the nurse if Danielle was still breathing on her own. She said, "No. Not any more." By that time she was showing four of the six signs which determined when a patient was brain dead.

All of the doctors (I don't know how many there were) called for a conference to let me know what was going on. In the conference room they explained what had happened and what was occurring then. They said that we could still have as much time with Danielle as we wanted. The doctors and nurses at that hospital did everything they could to make it easier for me. They were very compassionate and, even though they deal with that same thing every day, they still tried to help me the best they could.

When they asked me if I had any questions, I said, "Yes, how do I say goodbye to her?" I laid my head down on the table and sobbed. I just didn't know how to let her go. She had fought so hard and this is not fair.

THIS IS NOT FAIR!

Dr. Williams put his arms around me and hugged. All he could say was, "How did this happen?" Danielle's neurologist came in to see me, too. He had been called about a patient in ICU needing him and when he heard that it was Danielle, he dropped the phone. By that time all of the doctors knew her very well and every one of them had expected her to win over the aplastic anemia.

Another question I asked was if Danielle could be an organ donor. After all she had been in line to receive a bone marrow transplant, so maybe she could save someone else's life instead. The doctors were not sure about that but promised to check on it. It was possible that because of the disease and the chemicals used in her treatments, she might not be allowed to. It took them a couple of hours to find out that Danielle would only be able to donate her corneas. By that time I told the doctors that I was ready to let them take her off the life support.

All of us had to leave the room while they removed the respirator. No one knew how long Danielle would breathe on her own, or if she could at all. I only hoped that it would not be hours because I couldn't watch her struggle for air. I prayed, "Please, God, give her peace."

In a few moments they came to get us and we went to her room again. Danielle looked very peaceful, as if she was sleeping. I got on the bed and lay beside her. There were a few others in the room, including her nurse and a clergyman, but I didn't pay enough attention to know who else was there. All I could say to Danielle was, "I love you. I'm here." When I looked at her I noticed that her heart was beating so hard that I could see the pulse in her neck. It would beat a few times and pause, then it would do it again and pause. During the pauses I would tell her I loved her and then wait for the next beat. "She could be staying alive because she can hear me." I thought, "I don't want to hold her here and make her struggle longer." So I stayed quiet for a few minutes and the beats stopped. The clergyman said, "She is gone now." "I know," I whispered.

Just after Danielle took her last breath, I had second thoughts. "Oh, dear God, what have I done? Put the respirator on again. She's too strong to let go. Give her a couple more days." But I couldn't actually say anything because the words wouldn't come out. I just sobbed instead. The phone rang and I answered it. Mark was calling. I told him, She's gone. It happened just a few minutes ago."

I asked the nurse, "What do I do now?" She said that they would contact the funeral home for me. But, that wasn't what I meant when I asked the question. For the past year every aspect of my life was consumed with Danielle's illness and I was asking how I could let all that go and continue with my life. The nurse wanted to know if I would like to have a picture of Danielle. I told her that I already had a lot of other pictures—happier ones—of her at the hospital.

As I started to leave the ICU I walked by the plaque with the poem, "Know That I Am In Control." That time when I read it I replaced "him" with "her" and it made more sense to me. When I walked down the hallway I thought, "I'm never coming back here again. I'm leaving Danielle here and I'll never see this hospital again." My mind rebelled at the thought, "No, this isn't right. Boo is still here. I'll be calling tonight to tell her goodnight and that I love her just like every other time in the past."

When we were about half way home, the reality of the situation hit me in the pit of my stomach. I asked Alisha to pull off somewhere so that I could get something to eat or I was going to be sick. Terrible thoughts assailed me. "I can't believe what I have just done. I let her go without a fight. I'm a terrible mother. It's all my fault. I chose the chemotherapy, which led to the bleeding in her lung, which led to the weak spot in her brain, which bled when her platelets dropped too low. Then I made the ultimate decision to let her go. I gave up. If I made all the wrong decisions with Danielle, how could I be a good mother to Cole and Casey?" I watched people in other cars going by on the highway and thought, "Don't they understand that my world has just ended?" Danielle never had a chance to live so what was the sense of living?

There was a laundry basket of clean clothes on my bed when I got home. I started folding them while sitting on the bed and talking to some friends who had come to see me. I said to them, "What am I doing? I just lost Danielle and I'm folding clothes. I just don't know what to do now."

Chapter 42

The Funeral

Later that night I did feel a little better when I thought about Danielle being right there in Vassar, rather than being an hour and a half away. And, in spite of that, my thoughts went like this, "I need to call Danielle to wish her goodnight and tell her I love her." I really did know what had happened but just couldn't accept it. I still thought that I could go and see her or call her.

The first time I went to the funeral home I noticed a sign in front that said "Services for" and just below was "Danielle Tausch." Her name being on their sign really shook me up. I was there to pick out a casket and I did find one that I thought she would have liked. It was white with a purple lining. Purple was Danielle's favorite color. Her first showing was going to be the next day and I didn't know if I could stand seeing her in the casket. What was that going to be like? I was terribly lonely and I hurt so much. I realized that she was then perfect where she was and that she was once again whole, but I missed her so and still felt a lot of guilt. I would never hear her voice or touch her skin or see the Danielle that I once knew ever again.

The next day at the funeral home I hesitantly went through the doors into the room where Danielle was on view. From the entrance at the back of the room I could see the casket and the top of her head and I thought, "Do I <u>really</u> want to go the rest of the way? Do I want to know that it really <u>is</u> her in there?" I continued slowly and saw more and more of her as I got closer. She looked very peaceful, but she didn't look like Danielle to me. Her hair was curly and looked good but I was used to her with straight hair. She wore a pretty barrette in her hair and had polish on her nails, but her lips were swollen—probably from the medicines she had been taking.

All of a sudden I was angry! I didn't want anyone hugging or even touching me or to hear them say, "I'm so sorry." "Is there anything I can do?" or even, "How nice she looks." I was angry because Danielle was so young and because I caused her death. A mother is suppose to protect her children, not have to decide when to let them off life support. I failed Danielle, I made the wrong decisions. Others just could not understand how I felt.

The viewing lasted two days; the first was for the family only and the second was for everyone else. I stayed at the back of the room and didn't interact with others unless I had to. I saved my crying for when there was no one around and I could go to the casket and kiss Danielle or touch her hand. Even then I still had the urge to drive to the hospital to look for her.

On the third day the funeral itself was held at our church. I didn't look around, but someone told me that it was standing room only. It was almost overwhelming to see how many people Danielle touched in some way. I wish that she could have seen everyone that cared about her and came to say goodbye to her. The only things I remember from the service were my brother-in-law reading a poem, my cousin singing a song and a school friend of Danielle's reciting a poem for her.

When the ceremony ended everyone left but the family. Privately we would see Danielle one last time and say our goodbyes. I walked to the casket and looked down at her. Then I started to walk away, but instead I turned, bent down to kiss her forehead and began sobbing. Mom took my arm and led me outside to wait for the drive to the cemetery.

At the cemetery I heard someone say, "Well, she has other kids. Right?" What did that mean? Did it mean that this sort of thing was supposed to be easier because I had other children?—that I could use them to replace Danielle? Some people have very little compassion or understanding. Mark, his grandmother and a few others chose to stay, but I couldn't watch her being lowered into the ground. It was more than I could stand.

Epilogue

For a time I visited the cemetery every day because I just couldn't stand not knowing how Danielle was. I would talk to her and beg her to forgive me for the decisions I made. I pleaded with her and hoped that she understood. I was going crazy wondering if she were cold or needed anything. My mind told me she was in Heaven and perfect in every way but my heart told me that I was her mom and I should be taking care of her. For a while I even considered the idea of suicide so that I could find her and be with her. My grief was so overwhelming at times that I thought it would take over completely. Cole and Casey were what kept me going and what made me get out of bed each day.

About a week after Danielle passed away, a package came in the mail. After opening it, I found that it was the CD of her own song that we had ordered when she was in the hospital. Right away I put it in the player and listened to it. Danielle never was able to hear her song, but it was a great comfort to me. It was almost as if it had been made as much for me as for her.

It has been four years since those events took place. I deal with my grief better now and I can think of Danielle without crying and completely falling apart each time. I still can't forgive myself—I doubt if that guilt will ever go away. Once I even got up the nerve to visit the hospital—a small part of me was still looking for her. After leaving, I cried. It was like closing another door because Danielle was not there.

Every once in a while I hear about something that gives me a little bit of happiness. For instance, a while after Danielle passed away, I learned that the entire Vassar School basketball team drew her initials on their socks and wore them while playing a couple of their games. So many people supported Danielle in so many different ways. Her courage in fighting her battle touched the hearts of many people.

Grief makes you think many strange thoughts and it can drive you insane if you let it. I'm still here today only because of Cole and Casey. Sometimes I think back and remember the comment that was made at the funeral. Then I agree, "Yes, I do have other children, thanks be to God. He knew that I was going to need them."

There are many details to this story that I haven't told here but I have included most of it. In case it is ever published it will be because I want others to know that they are not alone when dealing with tragic situations. Maybe the person right next to you is suffering the same anxieties and grief that you are experiencing, but just isn't showing it in the same way. You must reach out to others and, just as importantly, be receptive when others reach out to you. Another piece of advice I would give anyone going through such a trial is to keep a journal. Write everything down as soon as it happens. Someday you will be looking through the journal and think, "Oh, yes, I forgot about that." A journal can hold so many memories.

A couple of times during the past four years, I started to write Danielle's story but couldn't finish it. I would get a little way into the first chapters and then break down. At that point I would walk away from it. Now, after four years, I have finally been able to get through it all the way to the end. The last chapters were the most difficult part of the story to experience over again. After it was finished I asked my cousin, Jerry Davis, if he would help me revise the story. He agreed to do it and, together, we spent several months editing the narrative into what it is today. Through that process I have gained a great friend.

About The Author

Shawn (Tausch) Williams was born at Ft. Knox, Kentucky in 1969 while her father was stationed there in the army. When she was only a few months old he was discharged and the family moved home to Michigan. Shawn attended elementary school there and graduated from Vassar High School during the spring of 1987.

After high school she attended Davenport University and became certified in the field of phlebotomy. She has been employed most of her career in some phase of the health care field. Presently she works part-time as an in-home care giver.

Shawn and her husband, Mark, were married in 1998 and now live in Vassar with their son, Cole, and daughter, Casey.

Printed in the United States
5003LVS00006B/22-27